A Slow Walk with Peter

A Slow Walk with Peter

275 Devotional Meditations

Edward B. Allen

Melbourne

A Slow Walk with Peter:
275 Devotional Meditations
by Edward B. Allen
Copyright © 2019 by Edward B. Allen
All rights reserved worldwide.
Reprinted with revisions, 2020, 2021, 2026.

Published by Edward B. Allen
Melbourne, Florida
Email: edward.allen1949@gmail.com

ISBN: 978-1-7333042-0-7 (paperback)
978-1-7320708-8-2 (standard ebook *.epub)
978-1-7320708-9-9 (Kindle ebook *.mobi)

Contact the publisher if you have questions regarding copying this book.

Scripture quotations marked CSB have been taken from the *Christian Standard Bible*®, Copyright © 2017 by Holman Bible Publishers. Used by permission. *Christian Standard Bible*® and CSB® are federally registered trademarks of Holman Bible Publishers.

Scripture versions are noted by the following abbreviations in this work.

> CSB, *Christian Standard Bible*, © 2017 Holman Bible Publishers
> KJV, *The Holy Bible*, King James Version, pubic domain
> NIV, *The Holy Bible, New International Version*, © 2011 Biblica Inc.

Cover design by Ken Raney (http://kenraney.com).

To Angie

Contents

Contents

Contents

Contents

Meditations on 2 Peter

Contents

Contents

Preface

Peter was one of Jesus' closest disciples. As one of the original apostles, he became a leader in the early church, eventually preaching in Rome where he was martyred. He wrote two general letters to first-century believers which have been embraced by Christians as part of the Bible. Peter wrote about a wide variety of topics including our hope in Christ, holy living, godly relationships, persecution, church leadership, false teachers, and Jesus' return. Jude, the brother of James and half-brother of Jesus, wrote a short letter to Christians warning them about ungodly people infiltrating local church congregations.

This book is a collection of devotional meditations, slowly walking through both letters from Peter, plus Jude's letter, a few verses at a time. The stories are based on the recollections of actual people and events by friends, family, or myself, unless otherwise indicated. Write your personal thoughts about the passage in the blank space at the bottom of most pages.

The *Christian Standard Bible* (CSB) is quoted as the primary translation of the Bible. It is a modern translation based on the latest evangelical scholarship. Clarifications of quotes are in [brackets]. Scripture references consist of book, chapter, verses, and version (if relevant), for example, "1 Peter 1:1 (CSB)." Cross-references to other Scriptures are in the notes. Transliterated Hebrew and Greek words are in *italics*, mostly in notes. Hebrew and Greek definitions are from Strong's *Exhaustive Concordance of the Bible.* Strong's reference numbers for Hebrew and Greek words are used rather than full citations, for example, "(*Strong's* No. 5360)." Some background comes from commentaries by Edwin A. Blum,[1] who is an evangelical Bible scholar. Addresses of Web sites are followed by dates when they were valid, for example, "(Current June 20, 2019)." All titles and Scripture references are indexed. A word or phrase referred to as a word is in *italics*. Male pronouns are sometimes used to indicate a person of either gender.

I thank my many Facebook friends for their encouraging responses to early drafts of these devotional meditations. I am also thankful for the support of my wife, Angie.

E.B.A.

---

[1]Edwin A. Blum, "1 Peter," "2 Peter," and "Jude," *The Expositor's Bible Commentary*, Vol. 12 (Grand Rapids, Michigan: Zondervan, 1981).

Meditations on 1 Peter

1 Foreigner

> Peter, an apostle of Jesus Christ: To those
> chosen, living as exiles dispersed abroad
> in Pontus, Galatia, Cappadocia, Asia,
> and Bithynia.
>
> 1 Peter 1:1 (CSB)

My family moved to Florida when I was just a few
weeks old, so I think of myself as a Floridian. I
like to say I've had Florida sand between my toes
all my life, so my feet keep going back there. But I
lived many years in northern states where it snows.
When I had to shovel snow, I felt like a foreigner,
far from my sunny homeland.

Peter wrote to persecuted believers who had
been scattered across most of modern Turkey—
exiles. I identify with those early Christians. Like
them, I'm not living in my spiritual homeland. This
world's system is not my home. It is the opposite of
God's kingdom.

> PRAYER: Lord, thank you for preparing
> a permanent home for me. Amen.

2 Scattered

> Peter, an apostle of Jesus Christ: To those
> chosen, living as exiles dispersed abroad
> in Pontus, Galatia, Cappadocia, Asia,
> and Bithynia.
>
> 1 Peter 1:1 (CSB)

Those Peter wrote to were not a big tight-knit community. There were small groups at best. Perhaps just a family or two in one place. They were dispersed.

I've often felt spiritually isolated on business trips. Coworkers weren't believers, the city was unfamiliar, and sometimes I didn't have a rental car. Even though there may be a church on the corner, it can be difficult to find those who love the Lord. God's people are scattered.

But on several business trips, my wife and I connected with home Bible studies. A referral from a friend or a little Internet research found a church that sponsored such groups. We treasured these opportunities to meet small groups of believers who have the same faith as we do.

> PRAYER: Lord, when I'm traveling, help me find those believers who love you. Amen.

PERSONAL THOUGHTS

3 Chosen

> [To God's chosen,] according to the fore-
> knowledge of God the Father, through
> the sanctifying work of the Spirit, to be
> obedient and to be sprinkled with the
> blood of Jesus Christ. May grace and
> peace be multiplied to you.
>
> 1 Peter 1:2 (CSB)

All the kids in the neighborhood had gathered to play softball. Two older kids were team captains. The rest of us stood there. One by one the captains picked their teams. Some were picked first; some were picked last; everybody got to play, even the little kids.

The Father has chosen me to be on his team. God is interested in me personally. The Father has known all about me from the beginning. My purpose is to do whatever Jesus says. Then I will be a success. I am able to do so, because his blood cleanses me from sin and the Holy Spirit has worked in my heart to make me special, pure for his use, serving him.

> PRAYER: Lord, thank you for choosing me to be on your team. Amen.

PERSONAL THOUGHTS

4 Foreknowledge

[To God's chosen,] according to the fore-
knowledge of God the Father, through
the sanctifying work of the Spirit, to be
obedient and to be sprinkled with the
blood of Jesus Christ. May grace and
peace be multiplied to you.

1 Peter 1:2 (CSB)

Mom was busy, not paying attention to the little boy
who was sneaking around the house. "Eddie, what
are you doing?" I wondered how she knew I was
into mischief. Did she have eyes in the back of her
head? Moms seem to know about the trouble little
boys can get into.

The creator of the universe is lord of time. God
the Father is not surprised by anything I might do.
He knew I would need salvation in the beginning.
He knows my whole story from beginning to end.

PRAYER: Lord, your knowledge about
my life is amazing. Thank you for car-
ing about me. Amen.

PERSONAL THOUGHTS

5 Set apart

> [To God's chosen,] according to the fore-
> knowledge of God the Father, through
> the sanctifying work of the Spirit, to be
> obedient and to be sprinkled with the
> blood of Jesus Christ. May grace and
> peace be multiplied to you.
>
> 1 Peter 1:2 (CSB)

When Grandmother passed away, Angie inherited
a steel serving spoon. It's ordinary. It didn't cost
much. Somehow the tip was broken off, so the
spoon has a flat side. This spoon has a special
purpose—to make tacos. When the tortilla comes
off the grill, this spoon with the flat side puts the
meat in the taco.

To *sanctify* means to set apart. The Holy Spirit is
working on my character so I can consistently live
like the citizen of the kingdom that I am. Even if I
have a flat side, I am set apart for his special pur-
poses.

> PRAYER: Lord, I confess that my charac-
> ter needs work. Thank you for setting
> me apart. Amen.

PERSONAL THOUGHTS

6   Obedient

> [To God's chosen,] according to the fore-
> knowledge of God the Father, through
> the sanctifying work of the Spirit, to be
> obedient and to be sprinkled with the
> blood of Jesus Christ. May grace and
> peace be multiplied to you.
>
> 1 Peter 1:2 (CSB)

When I was in Army Basic Training, I knew I had to instantly obey when the drill sergeant barked an order. There was no time for doubts and arguments. I also knew what the consequences would be if he had to tell me twice.

When Jesus says something, I want to obey the first time I hear it. The Sermon on the Mount[2] explains how to live as a citizen of the kingdom of heaven. I want to live that way without needing to be told again. The Love Chapter[3] tells me how to love. I want to love that way without needing to be told again.

> PRAYER: Lord, help me to be sensitive
> to your word, so that I instantly obey.
> Amen.

---

[2]Matthew 5:1–7:29.
[3]1 Corinthians 13:1–13.

7   Sprinkled

> [To God's chosen,] according to the fore-
> knowledge of God the Father, through
> the sanctifying work of the Spirit, to be
> obedient and to be sprinkled with the
> blood of Jesus Christ. May grace and
> peace be multiplied to you.
>
> 1 Peter 1:2 (CSB)

In ancient Israel, an item or person was sprinkled
with the blood of a sacrificed animal to ceremoni-
ally cleanse it from contaminating sin.[4]

When Jesus was on the cross, his back was
bleeding from the beating he endured. His head
was bleeding from the crown of thorns. His hands
and feet were bleeding from the nails. After he
died, a soldier put a spear into his side; blood and
water poured out. Jesus' death on the cross is why
I have been forgiven of my sins. Figuratively, I
have been "sprinkled with his blood" which means
I have been cleansed from contaminating sin.

> PRAYER: Lord, thank you for cleansing
> me from sin which contaminated my
> life. Amen.

---

[4]For example, Exodus 29:21.

8   Grace and peace

> [To God's chosen,] according to the fore-
> knowledge of God the Father, through
> the sanctifying work of the Spirit, to be
> obedient and to be sprinkled with the
> blood of Jesus Christ. May grace and
> peace be multiplied to you.
>
> 1 Peter 1:2 (CSB)

A little child knows who Dad is. He knows that
Dad gives him yummy food for breakfast and warm
clothes. He tells Dad all today's stories. He is free
to snuggle in Dad's arms and to sleep with Dad in
the big soft chair.

God loves me unconditionally. I have received
his grace. He has forgiven my sins, and he provides
for all my needs. I am confident he listens to me. I
have his peace deep inside. I rest in his love for me.
I know who I am—a child of the King.

> PRAYER: Lord, thank you for making me
> your child. Amen.

PERSONAL THOUGHTS

9 Praise

> Blessed be the God and Father of our Lord Jesus Christ. Because of his great mercy he has given us new birth into a living hope through the resurrection of Jesus Christ from the dead.
>
> 1 Peter 1:3 (CSB)

I like singing praises to God. "Praise God from whom all blessings flow" has a nice melody. The harmony is pretty. It's easy to concentrate on the music and forget why I'm singing.

God the Father has been very merciful to me. He's forgiven all my sin. I'm born again. Those are good reasons to sing his praises.

> PRAYER: Lord, I'll keep singing your praises, and I won't forget why I'm singing. Amen.

PERSONAL THOUGHTS

10   Living hope

> Blessed be the God and Father of our Lord Jesus Christ. Because of his great mercy he has given us new birth into a living hope through the resurrection of Jesus Christ from the dead.
>
> 1 Peter 1:3 (CSB)

Many people are discouraged, beat down by life's circumstances. They look for hope in surroundings, plans, and schemes. They may try to find a safe neighborhood. They may make big plans for a career. They may embrace get-rich-quick schemes. They don't know the hope that comes from within, from knowing Jesus.

I have hope for my future. My hope is not due to calculation, plans, or schemes. I have hope because Jesus rose from the dead. I know he is more powerful than any circumstance, even death. Death, the final enemy, was defeated. So I have entrusted my future to the victor—Jesus.

PRAYER: Lord, thank you for the hope you have given me. Amen.

PERSONAL THOUGHTS

11 Inheritance

> And [new birth] into an inheritance that
> is imperishable, undefiled, and unfad-
> ing, kept in heaven for you.
>
>   1 Peter 1:4 (CSB)

When my father died, I inherited his household
items. Time has passed and his potted plants have
died. The handle on his rake came off, and some of
his tools are rusty. His necktie and robe have faded.
A natural inheritance doesn't last forever.

I have become a child of God, adopted into his
family. There is an inheritance for me stored in his
presence. Nothing will have died. Nothing will
have rusted. Nothing will have faded. It will last
forever, in perfect condition.

PRAYER: Lord, thank you for the inheritance you have for me. Amen.

PERSONAL THOUGHTS

12   Guarded

> You are being guarded by God's power
> through faith for a salvation that is ready
> to be revealed in the last time.
>
> 1 Peter 1:5 (CSB)

In ancient times, a soldier's shield protected him from arrows. Sometimes the arrows were tipped with flaming rags soaked in oil. The arrows would just bounce off the shield.

I have a shield, namely, my faith in God's power and love.[5] God's power is what makes my shield strong. It does not prevent trials or persecution, but the shield does protect my soul from the attacks of Satan. My salvation is secure. When Jesus returns, my salvation will be obvious to all.

> PRAYER: Lord, thank you for guarding my soul through assurance of salvation. Amen.

PERSONAL THOUGHTS

---

[5]Ephesians 6:16.

13 Rejoice

You rejoice in this, even though now for
a short time, if necessary, you suffer grief
in various trials.

1 Peter 1:6 (CSB)

There are many reasons to smile. I can have fun
playing a game. I can bask in compliments from
those around me. I can admire beautiful surroundings. I can feel secure when the doors are locked.

But I am rejoicing, even though I face grief and
difficulties from time to time. I have an eternal
hope, an inheritance that does not rust, and a shield
of faith. My joy comes from deep inside. Daily life
sometimes has problems and disappointments, but
I'm rejoicing because I'm looking ahead to what's
coming.

PRAYER: Lord, thank you for all the reasons to rejoice that you have a given me.
Amen.

PERSONAL THOUGHTS

14   Faith

> So that the proven character of your
> faith—more valuable than gold which,
> though perishable, is refined by fire—
> may result in praise, glory, and honor at
> the revelation of Jesus Christ.
>
> 1 Peter 1:7 (CSB)

Faith is agreement with God that comes from deep
within—so deep that my life may be risked for the
gospel.

Faith is not intellectual assent to doctrines. Doctrine should be a summary of biblical teaching.
Doctrine is always formulated by people. Faith is
not repeating slogans, trying to convince myself. It
is not shouting louder, in case I didn't hear it the
first time. Faith is not trying to convince God to do
what I want.

Faith is knowing that God is good, that he loves
me, that he is all powerful, and that all doubts will
be settled when Jesus comes again.

> PRAYER: Lord, give me a deeper under-
> standing of genuine faith. Amen.

PERSONAL THOUGHTS

15　Gold

> So that the proven character of your
> faith—more valuable than gold which,
> though perishable, is refined by fire—
> may result in praise, glory, and honor at
> the revelation of Jesus Christ.
>
> 1 Peter 1:7 (CSB)

What can I buy with an ounce of gold? Can gold buy designer clothes, a big screen TV, or a luxury weekend get-away? Can gold buy joy? Can gold buy an eternal inheritance?

What can one make with an ounce of gold? One can make some shiny jewelry. One can make a wedding ring. They make electronics with gold contacts.

Can electronics compare to the power of God? Can a wedding ring make me a member of the Bride of Christ?[6] Can shiny jewelry reflect the glory of God? Faith is worth more than gold.

> PRAYER:　Lord, I will treasure faith
> in you above anything gold can buy.
> Amen.

PERSONAL THOUGHTS

---

[6]Ephesians 5:25–32 and Revelation 19:7–9.

16   Not seen

> Though you have not seen [Christ], you
> love him; though not seeing him now,
> you believe in him, and you rejoice with
> inexpressible and glorious joy.
>
> 1 Peter 1:8 (CSB)

I have some cousins whom I have never met in person, but I love them. I get letters from them. I see their Facebook posts. I know their parents. I rejoice with them when another baby is born.

Human relationships give us a glimpse of spiritual relationships. The disciple Thomas got to put his finger in Jesus' nail-scarred hand.[7] I don't need to do so, because I believe Thomas' testimony—Jesus is alive! I love Jesus because he first loved me. Believing in Jesus makes me so happy I can't describe it.

> PRAYER: Lord, I believe the testimony of
> those who saw you in person. Amen.

PERSONAL THOUGHTS

---

[7]John 20:26–29.

17 Salvation

> Because you are receiving the goal of
> your faith, the salvation of your souls.
>
> 1 Peter 1:9 (CSB)

When my friend promises to buy me lunch next week, I'll arrive at the restaurant on time, because I believe he will fulfill in his promise. How much more should I have faith in God's promise of salvation?

I clearly remember the night I received the eternal salvation of my soul at a children's camp. The preacher asked if anyone had not asked Jesus into his heart. I responded. Afterward, a camp counselor explained the gospel to me. I believed and that was it. I felt wonderful.

> PRAYER: Lord, thank you for the salvation of my soul. Amen.

PERSONAL THOUGHTS

18   Included

> Concerning this salvation, the prophets,
> who prophesied about the grace that
> would come to you, searched and care-
> fully investigated.
>
> 1 Peter 1:10 (CSB)

Each piece of a jigsaw puzzle reveals only a small bit of the whole picture. As they come together, one corner might make sense. If you let me look at the box cover, then the mystery is solved and all the pieces will fall in place.

The Old Testament prophets foretold elements of God's plan of salvation, but they could not see the whole picture. Early Jewish Christians were very surprised that salvation was a gift of God to the Gentiles, too—people like me. We read about Peter and Cornelius, a Roman soldier,[8] Philip and the Ethiopian eunuch,[9] and Paul's travels throughout the Roman empire.[10]   Yes, Gentiles are included.

God's forgiveness, his grace, is available to anyone. It is not limited to just one nationality. God wants all to repent and receive his offer of salvation.

> PRAYER: Lord, I'm thankful to be included in your salvation. Amen.

---

[8] Acts 10:1–48.

[9] Acts 8:26–40.

[10] Acts chapters 13–28.

19   When?

> [The prophets] inquired into what time
> or what circumstances the Spirit of
> Christ within them was indicating when
> he testified in advance to the sufferings
> of Christ and the glories that would fol-
> low.
>
> 1 Peter 1:11 (CSB)

When our family traveled, we kids wanted to know
"When will get there, Dad?" Dad may have known
it would be another half an hour, but he didn't tell
us. When we saw Grandma's house it was obvious
we were there.

Even though the Old Testament prophets were
eager to know when the Messiah was coming, God
kept it secret until Jesus came. God's plan then became obvious. Jesus suffered an agonizing death on
the cross for my sins and then rose from the dead to
reign as king of the universe. God chose the time
and circumstances of the Messiah's coming. Now,
understanding the events of the gospel does not require any special prophetic gift, knowledge, or ed-
ucation.

> PRAYER: Lord, thank you for revealing
> your plan. Amen.

20   Convinced

> It was revealed to [the prophets] that they were not serving themselves but you. These things have now been announced to you through those who preached the gospel to you by the Holy Spirit sent from heaven—angels long to catch a glimpse of these things.
>
> 1 Peter 1:12 (CSB)

When I was a young Christian, I was fascinated by Bible prophecy. I studied Old Testament predictions about the Messiah. Did the Jesus fulfill those predictions? I studied end-times Bible passages and read books about the second coming of Jesus. Is Jesus coming soon? What will happen when he comes?

I saw how the life, death, and resurrection of Jesus fulfilled many Old Testament prophecies. I was convinced. Jesus is the Messiah. That gives me confidence that the rest of the predictions about the Messiah's kingdom will also happen—perhaps within my lifetime.

PRAYER: Come, Lord Jesus! Amen.

PERSONAL THOUGHTS

21   Alert

> Therefore, with your minds ready for action, be sober-minded and set your hope completely on the grace to be brought to you at the revelation of Jesus Christ.
>
> 1 Peter 1:13 (CSB)

Whenever my spoon went "clink" on the bottom of my ice-cream dish our Yorkshire terrier was ready for action. He was hoping to lick the bowl. His tongue was long enough to reach the bottom. No ice-cream opportunity was going to escape his attention. He was alert.

My hope is alert for the second coming of Jesus. When he returns, everyone will know that he is the rightful king of the universe. Everyone will see he is the almighty God. Everyone will find out he is the righteous judge. Because I'm God's child, I'll receive the grace that my faith is looking for. I am alert.

PRAYER: Lord, I am eager to see the return of Jesus to Planet Earth. Amen.

PERSONAL THOUGHTS

22   Grace

> Therefore, with your minds ready for action, be sober-minded and set your hope completely on the grace to be brought to you at the revelation of Jesus Christ.
>
> 1 Peter 1:13 (CSB)

Grace is defined as favor, especially from a superior. As a teacher, I liked to design exams so the correct answers were short phrases in English. When I graded the exams, the students' answers never matched my answer key. Sometimes there were synonyms, sometimes a vague phrase, and sometimes slang. I wanted to give credit for what each student knew. As I graded, I had to extend grace.

When Jesus comes again, I will receive grace. The dead in Christ will be resurrected and we who are alive will be changed into resurrection bodies like the Lord had on Easter morning.[11]

PRAYER: Lord, my hope is in your grace. Amen.

PERSONAL THOUGHTS

---

[11] 1 Thessalonians 4:13–18.

23 Not independent

> As obedient children, do not be con-
> formed to the desires of your former ig-
> norance.
>
> 1 Peter 1:14 (CSB)

Americans celebrate "independence." Our national
holiday is "Independence Day." The pioneers of the
old West are romanticized for their ability to make a
life without help from anyone—independence. The
national character says, "Don't tell me what to do!"
—independence. Americans don't like to be bossed
around—not by the government, not by neighbors,
and not by family.

Who do I think knows what is best for me? Me
or my heavenly Father? God knows me better than
I know myself. God knows what the future holds
and he knows what is right and pure. Even though
I'm an American, if Father knows best, then I had
better obey him.

> PRAYER: Lord, instead of being inde-
> pendent, help me be an obedient child.
> Amen.

PERSONAL THOUGHTS

24   Selfish desires

> As obedient children, do not be con-
> formed to the desires of your former ig-
> norance.
>
> 1 Peter 1:14 (CSB)

Temptations are everywhere in modern life. Adver-
tising is in your face, pushing greed, vanity, and
sex. Celebrities parade their immorality, and the
tabloids dutifully report them. The prevailing attitude is, "I'll do whatever I want." Selfishness rules.
Everyone has different desires, but all selfishness is
evil.

Because of Christ, I can't live like that any more.
The temptations are still there, but I must not be
molded into the world's selfish pattern. The Holy
Spirit gives me insight to see how foolish worldly
ways are, and how much better living in the kingdom of God is.

PRAYER: Lord, help me reject selfish desires and temptations. Amen.

PERSONAL THOUGHTS

25 Holy

> But as the one who called you is holy,
> you also are to be holy in all your con-
> duct.
>
> 1 Peter 1:15 (CSB)

Like every teenager, I wanted to be liked and accepted by my peers. Most teenagers are careful to
conform to the style of their friends—clothes, activ-
ities, slang, and so on. It was hard to let the real me
out, because I was so busy maintaining my mask.

I was a Christian well before I became a teenager. I knew the Lord expected me to live his holy
lifestyle and not do what my worldly friends did.
Those teen years were awkward, but I learned to
just be myself.

> PRAYER: Lord, help me to be the person
> you want me to be. Amen.

PERSONAL THOUGHTS

26   Family resemblance

> For it is written, "Be holy, because I am
> holy."
>
> 1 Peter 1:16 (CSB)

When I was a teenager, people would see me from
a distance and think I was my Dad. We were the
same height. Our heads had the same shape. We
both had dark hair and we both wore glasses. We
looked alike.

The Lord is holy! He is completely different
from sinful mankind. He is good. He is righteous.
He is wise. He is spirit, not flesh. He has given me
the ability to be holy like him, like I resembled my
Dad. I am God's representative, so I should reflect
his character. My reflection of him may be the only
way some people get to see him.

PRAYER: Lord, help me reflect your character. Amen.

PERSONAL THOUGHTS

27   Impartial

> If you appeal to the Father who judges
> impartially according to each one's
> work, you are to conduct yourselves
> in reverence during your time living as
> strangers.
>
> 1 Peter 1:17 (CSB)

When I grade term papers, I ask myself questions as
I read. Does the paper fulfill the assignment? Are
the ideas accurate? Is the explanation clear? I must
be impartial. Judging a term paper is hard. Which
ones deserve an A?

On the Last Day, God will judge what each person has done.[12] Was that action selfish? Was it
godly, pure, and righteous? Was that word gentle
and kind? There will be no excuses. He will be fair
and impartial. Therefore, I'll be careful with my attitudes and actions.

> PRAYER: Lord, I want my life to fulfill your assignment to me—an A grade.
> Amen.

PERSONAL THOUGHTS

---

[12] 2 Corinthians 5:10 and Revelation 20:11–13.

28   Reverence

> If you appeal to the Father who judges
> impartially according to each one's
> work, you are to conduct yourselves
> in reverence during your time living as
> strangers.
>
> 1 Peter 1:17 (CSB)

Even though I lived in a small town with little traffic, I was afraid every time I went out driving. I
knew that a careless moment by me or someone else
could result in an accident. That fear was a motivator to be watchful, to obey the law, and to make sure
my reactions were right.

Reverence is motivated by fear. When I read
about God's righteousness, I am afraid. I know my
actions are not always pure by his standards. His
righteousness is a motivator to be careful, to obey
his Word, and to make sure my heart is right. When
I do fall, I know his forgiveness is always available,
if I will go to him.

> PRAYER: Lord, I will conduct myself in
> reverence, because you are righteous.
> Amen.

PERSONAL THOUGHTS

29   Stranger

> If you appeal to the Father who judges
> impartially according to each one's
> work, you are to conduct yourselves
> in reverence during your time living as
> strangers.
>
> 1 Peter 1:17 (CSB)

I had a summer job in Germany. I hardly spoke
any German. Going to the grocery store was a vo-
cabulary lesson. The supervisor at work and other
Germans I met who spoke English were not believers. I felt isolated socially and spiritually. I was a
stranger.

Worldly folks speak a different language than I
do. They use profanity, obscenity, sexual innuendo,
and vulgarity. Their values are different from the
kingdom of God. I can get along in a secular work
environment, but socializing is difficult and super-
ficial.

> PRAYER: Lord, I feel like a stranger in
> this world. Amen.

PERSONAL THOUGHTS

30 Legal tender

> For you know that you were redeemed
> from your empty way of life inherited
> from your fathers, not with perishable
> things like silver or gold.
>
> 1 Peter 1:18 (CSB)

At the international airport terminal, there is a booth where you can exchange your dollars for some other currency. Every country has its own type of money: dollars, euros, yen, and so on. A dollar bill says "This note is legal tender for all debts, public and private." Coins used to be made of gold and silver. Gold bars were kept in government vaults to back up money.

However, money nor gold bars nor silver coins will pay the debt for an empty way of life. An empty life may be traditional. An empty life may be what is advertised on TV, but I needed redemption from sin. No country's money could pay that debt. I have been redeemed by the blood of Jesus who died on the cross for the sins of all mankind.

PRAYER: Lord, thank you for redeeming
me from an empty life. Amen.

PERSONAL THOUGHTS

31   Way of life

> For you know that you were redeemed
> from your empty way of life inherited
> from your fathers, not with perishable
> things like silver or gold.
>
> 1 Peter 1:18 (CSB)

What is the way of life that I have inherited? Western civilization is my heritage. Like many other
civilizations, Western civilization is very materialis-
tic. Even though Christianity has influenced Western civilization, its roots were in pagan Greece and
Rome. More recently, the Enlightenment period
made atheism an acceptable part of Western civilization.

I have received an empty way of life from Western civilization. I treasure the godly influence of
some of my ancestors, but all around me is the spiritual emptiness of Western civilization. I have a new
way of life based on knowing Jesus and doing what
the Bible teaches. The kingdom of heaven is my
new civilization.

> PRAYER: Lord, thank you for giving me
> a new way of life. Amen.

PERSONAL THOUGHTS

32 Blood

> But [redeemed] with the precious blood
> of Christ, like that of an unblemished
> and spotless lamb.
>
> 1 Peter 1:19 (CSB)

Without blood, I cannot live. My blood carries the nutrients of life to every tiny cell of my body. The oxygen I breath, the food I eat, and cells that fight disease all find their way and are carried along by the blood.

Without the blood of Jesus, I cannot live. His blood paid for my redemption from sin. His Word feeds my soul. The Holy Spirit in me is the breath of a full life. By his blood, forgiveness for every tiny sin is available to me. By his blood, I receive healing and victory over death.

PRAYER: Lord, thank you for shedding your blood on the cross. Amen.

PERSONAL THOUGHTS

33 Lamb

> But [redeemed] with the precious blood
> of Christ, like that of an unblemished
> and spotless lamb.
>
> 1 Peter 1:19 (CSB)

In ancient Israel, a sacrifice for sin had to be a lamb that was perfect. The lamb could not be sick or injured. The wool had to be white, not spotted or black. Nothing could symbolize contamination by sin. The sacrifice had to qualify as a substitute for sinners.

John the Baptist called Jesus the Lamb of God.[13] Jesus was fully human yet without sin. He was not contaminated by his own sin. He was fully qualified to be the substitute for sinners.

> PRAYER: Lord, thank you for dying for
> me, so that the penalty for my sins is
> paid. Amen.

PERSONAL THOUGHTS

---

[13]John 1:29.

34 Planning

> [Christ] was foreknown before the foundation of the world but was revealed in these last times for you.
>
> 1 Peter 1:20 (CSB)

When my wife and I expect to make a major purchase, we make plans well in advance. We look at our savings and our budget. We shop for the best price. We find out who has exactly the right model. When the time is right, we buy the item.

God was not surprised by the Fall of Adam and Eve.[14] He was not surprised by my sin. Before the universe was created, God had a plan to pay for my redemption. He knew the price was the death of a sinless man. The Son knew his mission. When the time was right, Jesus was born. God had a plan from the beginning.

> PRAYER: Lord, thank you for planning my salvation from the beginning. Amen.

PERSONAL THOUGHTS

---

[14]Genesis 3:1–24.

35   Revealed

> [Christ] was foreknown before the foundation of the world but was revealed in these last times for you.
>
> 1 Peter 1:20 (CSB)

The box was wrapped in shiny red and green paper. The ribbon around it was fastened with a bow. The tag said it was for me. However, I was not allowed to open it yet. Finally, the big day arrived. The tree in the living room was decorated with lights and ornaments. I retrieved the box from under the tree, and unwrapped it. Its secret was revealed.

Prophets hinted at the plan. The night Jesus was born, the angels announced the Messiah's arrival to the shepherds. A few weeks later, Simeon and Anna held him in their arms and told anyone who would listen that the Messiah was here. Later, magi from the East said a star announced the coming of the King of the Jews. The preaching of John the Baptist prepared people for the Messiah's message. God revealed his plan for the salvation of mankind. He waited until just the right time in history.

PRAYER: Lord, thank you for revealing your plan at just the right time. Amen.

PERSONAL THOUGHTS

36 Believe

> Through [Christ] you believe in God,
> who raised him from the dead and gave
> him glory, so that your faith and hope
> are in God.
>
> 1 Peter 1:21 (CSB)

Who can I trust to tell me the truth? Mom and Dad?
Teachers? The news media? Politicians? A used-car
salesman? People are not always reliable. I must
carefully evaluate what I read and hear. Knowing
the truth and knowing who to trust are important.

I believe God. I believe him when he says Jesus
rose from the dead. I believe him when he tells me
he loves me. I believe him when he points out my
sin. I believe him when he forgives me. I believe
him when he promises that I can live with him forever.

PRAYER: Lord, I believe what you say.
Amen.

PERSONAL THOUGHTS

37   Resurrection

> Through [Christ] you believe in God,
> who raised him from the dead and gave
> him glory, so that your faith and hope
> are in God.
>
> 1 Peter 1:21 (CSB)

Some people claim that all religions are the same. They say, "Each offers a way to eternal bliss. Each has a founding teacher. Take your pick. It doesn't matter which one you choose." Such a person is probably an atheist. It doesn't matter which religion you choose if God is not there.

Christianity is different. God raised Jesus from the dead in a glorified body that will never die. This confirmed that Jesus is king of the universe. It does matter whom you worship, because an almighty God really is there.

PRAYER: Lord, I know you are there, because Jesus rose from the dead. Amen.

PERSONAL THOUGHTS

38   Hope

> Through [Christ] you believe in God,
> who raised him from the dead and gave
> him glory, so that your faith and hope
> are in God.
>
> 1 Peter 1:21 (CSB)

Do you want to know the future? Some people read the horoscope in the newspaper. Some eagerly break fortune cookies. Some consult an astrologer. Some play the lottery, hoping for a jackpot. Some just hope everything will turn out okay.

I know everything will end up okay, because my hope is in God. He knows the whole story from beginning to end. He is not surprised by the twists and turns of my life. Jesus rose from the dead in an immortal body demonstrating his power. His love for me is the guarantee that I will live with him forever.

PRAYER: Lord, thank you for a guaranteed future. Amen.

PERSONAL THOUGHTS

39   Brotherly love

> Since you have purified yourselves by
> your obedience to the truth, so that you
> show sincere brotherly love for each
> other, from a pure heart love one an-
> other constantly.
>
> 1 Peter 1:22 (CSB)

Marcia is my only sibling. Our natural love for each
other developed as we grew up together. When
Marcia married, Tom was added to my circle of
brotherly love. When I married, Angie was added
to Marcia's circle of brotherly love. As Marcia's
children grew, Angie and I developed relationships
with them, an expanded circle of natural familial
brotherly love.

Brotherly love among Christians is also a natural result of our relationships with the heavenly Father. I am a child of God and you are a child of God,
so we are all in his family. Obeying the Word of God
in our relationship produces brotherly love. Godly
relationships confirm we are in the same family in
the Lord. I must treat other believers with love and
respect, because I must spend eternity with them. I
don't want anything I do in this life to hinder our
fellowship around the throne in heaven.

> PRAYER: Lord, help me love all my
> fellow believers like I love my family.
> Amen.

40   Love from a pure heart

> Since you have purified yourselves by
> your obedience to the truth, so that you
> show sincere brotherly love[15] for each
> other, from a pure heart love[16] one an-
> other constantly.
>
>   1 Peter 1:22 (CSB)

The gentleman hurried ahead to open the restaurant door for his family. He held it open for the elderly couple coming the other way. Then came another family. While his family waited, he held the
door for yet another couple. It may not have been
convenient, but he demonstrated love to people he
had never met.

Jesus demonstrated his love for me even though
we had never met. He showed self-sacrificing love.
Such love is more than being polite. It is more than
brotherly love, because it is applicable even to those
whom I don't know. It flows from a pure heart deep
within, because it is a fruit of the Holy Spirit in my
life.[17]

> PRAYER: Lord, give me self-sacrificing
> love for those around me, even those I
> don't know. Amen.

---

[15]The Greek word *philadelphia* (*Strong's* No. 5360).

[16]The Greek word *agapao* (*Strong's* No. 25).

[17]Galatians 5:22.

41 Born again

> You have been born again—not of perishable seed but of imperishable— through the living and enduring word of God.
>
> 1 Peter 1:23 (CSB)

When I was a kid, we planted seeds in a little cup, watered it, put it in the sunshine. Then we watched for the first sign of life. When God's truth was planted in me, new life sprouted, like the seeds in that cup.

I was ten years old at a Christian camp. The preacher in the chapel service explained that a personal commitment is necessary to get to heaven. I didn't remember ever doing that. A camp counselor explained the gospel. So I repented of my sin and asked Jesus into my life. I could tell that this was a new start to my life. I was born again.

PRAYER: Lord, thank you for my new life. Amen.

PERSONAL THOUGHTS

42 Not perishable seed

> You have been born again—not of
> perishable seed but of imperishable—
> through the living and enduring word
> of God.
>
> 1 Peter 1:23 (CSB)

I've been wondering what kinds of flowers to plant
in the backyard. One category is called *annuals* and
another is called *perennials*. Annuals are beautiful
for one season, but the plant dies when it becomes
too hot or too cold. Perennials bloom year after
year. Their lives are suited to the changing seasons.

A person's natural life lasts a limited number
of years. Body parts get old, wear out, and eventually fail. Death is the natural result, like an annual flower. When I was born again, my life gained
a perennial quality, because I have been promised
eternal life. My natural body may wear out and decay, but my resurrected body will be imperishable.
The source of my eternal life was God's promise.

PRAYER: Lord, thank you for your
promises which last forever. Amen.

PERSONAL THOUGHTS

43   Glory is like grass

> All flesh is like grass,
> and all its glory like a flower
> of the grass.
> The grass withers, and the
> flower falls,
> but the word of the Lord en-
> dures forever.

And this word is the gospel that was
proclaimed to you.

1 Peter 1:24–25 (CSB)

The football player ran for a touchdown. A hundred thousand fans in the stadium cheered. Mil-
lions heard his name on TV. The next week no one
remembered what he had done. Human glory is
fleeting. Emperors may build monuments to themselves, but in time, they crumble and we wonder,
"Who built that?"

The Word of God that I received when I was
born again is different. The Word of God is true
forever. It will always be active in my life. Receiv-
ing the Word of God did not stop when I was born
again. I've been learning God's Word ever since. It
makes life richer and richer. Those lessons will last
forever.

PRAYER: Lord, thank you for your Word.
Help me learn its lessons. Amen.

1 Peter 2:1

44 Malice

> Therefore, rid yourselves of all malice,
> all deceit, hypocrisy, envy, and all slan-
> der.
>
> 1 Peter 2:1 (CSB)

Dictionary.com defines *malice* as "the desire to in-
flict injury, harm or suffering on another either because of a hostile impulse or out of deep-seated
meanness." Malice is very common in modern society. Some people rejoice when someone else suffers.
Some people have hostility just below the surface,
ready to explode at anyone from the slightest trigger.

I should be driven by love rather than hostility
or meanness. I can't continue to embrace my old
hostile attitudes. I can't live with patterns of malice
anymore. Now that God has saved me and forgiven
me, I don't have a reason to hold onto hostility and
meanness.

PRAYER: Lord, help me replace malice
with love. Amen.

PERSONAL THOUGHTS

45 Deceit

> Therefore, rid yourselves of all malice,
> all deceit, hypocrisy, envy, and all slan-
> der.
>
> 1 Peter 2:1 (CSB)

Dictionary.com defines *deceit* as "the act or practice of deceiving; concealment or distortion of the truth for the purpose of misleading." Truth seems to be in short supply in modern society. We don't expect a politician, a lawyer, or a used-car salesman to tell the truth. Even journalists have lost their credibility. "Little white lies" are acceptable. Clothes and hairstyles, makeup and tatoos, cars and golf clubs are all ways to make a statement saying, "This image is who I am," hiding the real person. Even though Western culture claims truth as an ideal, reality falls far short.

God does not lie. Now that I am born again, I must become like my Father by getting rid of deceit. My whole lifestyle must reflect the truth. It starts with what I say with my mouth and extends to letting others know who I really am. Because God loves me, I don't need to hide who I am.

> PRAYER: Lord, thank you for the confi-
> dence to live without pretending to be
> someone else. Amen.

46 Hypocrisy

> Therefore, rid yourselves of all malice,
> all deceit, hypocrisy, envy, and all slan-
> der.
>
> 1 Peter 2:1 (CSB)

Dictionary.com defines *hypocrisy* as "a pretense of having a virtuous character, moral or religious beliefs or principles, etc. that one does not really possess." In America, a large majority identify as "Christian," but most ignore many clear teachings of the Bible. Even among those who attend church regularly, there are many who do not have a personal relationship with the Lord. *Christian* has become merely a cultural tag for many.

If I would lead an honest lifestyle as a believer, I must live obediently as I grow in my understanding of the Bible. I am trying to do what the Bible teaches, but I know I am not perfect in my obedience. Getting rid of hypocrisy means diligently seeking virtuous character, while acknowledging human frailty.

> PRAYER: Lord, I confess I don't always obey you. Help me follow your Word more consistently. Amen.

PERSONAL THOUGHTS

47   Envy

> Therefore, rid yourselves of all malice,
> all deceit, hypocrisy, envy, and all slan-
> der.
>
> 1 Peter 2:1 (CSB)

Dictionary.com defines *envy* as "a feeling of discontent or covetousness with regard to another's advantages, success, possessions, and so on." Most people consider envy normal. Some politicians even cultivate envy among voters. For example, "tax the rich" appeals to those who are not rich. This is envy at work. Occasions for envy pop up every day.

A coworker of mine was promoted to department manager. I rationalized: I was better qualified; I had seniority; I would do a great job. But in the end, I had to do what this verse teaches, get rid of envy.

> PRAYER: Lord, help me recognize envy
> in my attitudes, so I can repent and get
> rid of it. Amen.

PERSONAL THOUGHTS

48   Slander

> Therefore, rid yourselves of all malice,
> all deceit, hypocrisy, envy, and all slan-
> der.
>
> 1 Peter 2:1 (CSB)

Dictionary.com defines *slander* as "defamation,
calumny." *Defamation*, in turn, is defined as "false
or unjustified injury of the good reputation of another." *Calumny*, in turn, is defined as "a false or
malicious statement designed to injure the reputation of someone."

For example, on game day, the fans in the stadium heaped insults on the opposing football team.
Or in my college dorm, we played Hearts late into
the night; winners insulted losers. As I've grown as
a Christian, I've learned to not let competition de-
generate into slander. The Word teaches me to love
my enemies[18] and that includes the opposing football team and the other side in a card game.

> PRAYER: Lord, help me guard what I say,
> so no slander comes out. Amen.

PERSONAL THOUGHTS

---

[18]Matthew 5:44.

49   Milk

> Like newborn infants, desire the pure
> milk of the word, so that you may grow
> up into your salvation.
>
> 1 Peter 2:2 (CSB)

When I was a young Christian, I couldn't get
enough Bible study. As a teenager, it took me a couple of years to read through the Bible, but I made it
all the way, even through the boring parts. In college, discussion Bible studies became my favorite.
I've grown the most when I could talk about the
Word with others.

I need more spiritual milk. Recently my Bible
reading has been pretty erratic. I'm resolved to read
more, dig deeper, and grow more. The rush of daily
life won't crowd out the Word of God anymore.

PRAYER: Lord, forgive me for ignoring
your Word. Amen.

PERSONAL THOUGHTS

50   Growing up

> Like newborn infants, desire the pure
> milk of the word, so that you may grow
> up into your salvation.
>
> 1 Peter 2:2 (CSB)

When I received Jesus into my life at a young age,
I knew I was going to heaven, but I soon found out
living the Jesus way means growing in him. For me,
growing spiritually has been a gradual process, just
like growing up as a person.

Salvation is more than a ticket to heaven. Salvation means living as a citizen of heaven while here
on Planet Earth. It is taking a while for the various
areas of my life to exhibit God's salvation, but I'm
more radical for Jesus now than I've ever been.

PRAYER: Lord, help me to grow up into
a mature Christian. Amen.

PERSONAL THOUGHTS

51 Tasted

You have tasted that the Lord is good.
1 Peter 2:3 (CSB)

The first time I tasted a fresh mango I thought, "This is different. Sweet with a distinctive flavor." Now I have two large mango trees in the back yard. First one tree ripens its fruit and then the other. There will be plenty for us, the neighbors, and of course, the raccoons and squirrels.

When I first experienced God working in my life, I knew that he is good. As he has intervened in my circumstances, my faith has grown. As I share my stories with my neighbors, they will find out there is plenty of God's goodness for everyone, even for the raccoons and squirrels.

PRAYER: Lord, thank you for the good things you do in my life. Amen.

PERSONAL THOUGHTS

52 Come

As you come to [the Lord], a living
stone—rejected by people but chosen
and honored by God.

1 Peter 2:4 (CSB)

Daddy holds out his hands. Baby takes an unsteady
step or two. "Come to Daddy." Baby takes another step and falls down on his bottom. "Come to
Daddy." Baby gets up and takes the last few steps
to Daddy's open arms.

Growing up in the Lord means coming to my
heavenly Father, coming to Jesus, and welcoming
the Holy Spirit into my life. *Coming* means prayer,
worship, and obedience. I pray over everything in
life. I worship from the heart. I obey what I learn
from the Bible. The result is spiritual maturity.

PRAYER: Lord, I am coming to you with
all my concerns. Amen.

PERSONAL THOUGHTS

53 Rejected

> As you come to [the Lord], a living
> stone—rejected by people but chosen
> and honored by God.
>
> 1 Peter 2:4 (CSB)

In my neighborhood, an old tree died. A big ugly
stump was all that was left. Some people would
have planted grass there, but this homeowner called a guy with a chain saw who went to work. Before you knew it, two cute bear cubs climbing on a
tree were in front of the house. The ugly stump had
been transformed into a precious sculpture.

Jesus was rejected by people, especially the religious leaders, but God had a plan. Jesus' self sacrifice was precious to the Father. The Son of God was
the chosen Lamb of God, who paid for the sins of
the world, the honored Messiah.

PRAYER: Lord, thank you for paying for
my sins. Amen.

PERSONAL THOUGHTS

54 Under construction

> You yourselves, as living stones, a spir-
> itual house, are being built to be a holy
> priesthood to offer spiritual sacrifices ac-
> ceptable to God through Jesus Christ.
>
> 1 Peter 2:5 (CSB)

A construction site is an amazing place. People and machines going here and there. Stuff is being deliv-ered and trash is being carried away. It looks like chaos, but somehow a beautiful building emerges.

I'm like a stone at God's construction site. There is a flurry of activity. New stones are arriving. My trash is being carried away. I can't see the master plan, but God is the architect. He won't stop un-til his dwelling is complete with every stone in its proper place.

> PRAYER: Lord, I submit to your construc-
> tion project. I'm a stone in your spiritual
> house. Amen.

PERSONAL THOUGHTS

55   Living stones

> You yourselves, as living stones, a spiritual house, are being built to be a holy priesthood to offer spiritual sacrifices acceptable to God through Jesus Christ.
>
> 1 Peter 2:5 (CSB)

When my wife and I were dating, people would say, "Oh, you both play guitar—how romantic." Well, nothing could be further from the truth. We knew many of the same songs, but we each played them in different styles, in different keys, with slightly different chords, and we would sing slightly different words. Whenever we tried to play together, it was very stressful. But after all these years of married life, we have learned to play together. It took some time for our rough edges to get smoothed so we fit together.

The Holy Spirit is like a master mason who knows how each stone will fit among the others. He smooths some rough edges on this stone and that, so there is no gap between them. It may not feel good to have a sharp chip knocked off, but it is necessary. In the end, God's house will fit together perfectly.

PRAYER: Lord, thank you for shaping me to fit with other believers. Amen.

56   Priests

> You yourselves, as living stones, a spiritual house, are being built to be a holy priesthood to offer spiritual sacrifices acceptable to God through Jesus Christ.
>
>   1 Peter 2:5 (CSB)

In ancient Israel, priests were intermediaries between God and the people. They served God in the temple and offered sacrifices on behalf of the people. Although we no longer sacrifice animals, all Christians are qualified to offer spiritual sacrifices on behalf of others.

Today, I can be an intercessor, praying for others. I can pray for healing. I can pray for restored relationships. I can pray for provision of resources. I can pray for God to intervene in seemingly impossible situations. It's not hard to perform a priestly function. It starts on my knees with love for others.

PRAYER: Lord, thank you for answering my prayers for others. Amen.

PERSONAL THOUGHTS

57 Offerings

> You yourselves, as living stones, a spiritual house, are being built to be a holy priesthood to offer spiritual sacrifices acceptable to God through Jesus Christ.
>
> 1 Peter 2:5 (CSB)

My wife and I like to play our guitars and sing praises to the Lord. It is a simple thing. Sometimes we play in our living room, sometimes in a home Bible study, and sometimes at church.

We are glad when others join us in corporate praise, but we try to ignore what other people think. We are not performing for an audience. The only person listening who counts is the Lord, and he listens to our hearts. Praising God is an example of offering a spiritual sacrifice.[19]

PRAYER: Lord, I will praise you with my whole heart. Amen.

PERSONAL THOUGHTS

---

[19]Hebrews 13:15.

58   Spiritual sacrifices

> You yourselves, as living stones, a spiritual house, are being built to be a holy priesthood to offer spiritual sacrifices acceptable to God through Jesus Christ.
>
> 1 Peter 2:5 (CSB)

Being generous is more than contributing money to a good cause. I have found generosity includes giving household items to friends who can use them. I started by giving away small things. I discovered I didn't need those items anyway. A few times, I've given away a car. It is rewarding to see someone else enjoy those items.

God was generous to me when he sent his son. I can imitate him by being generous to others. Living a generous lifestyle is an example of offering spiritual sacrifices.

PRAYER: Lord, show me opportunities to be generous. Amen.

PERSONAL THOUGHTS

59   Cornerstone

For it stands in Scripture:

> See, I lay a stone in Zion,
> a chosen and honored corner-
> stone,
> and the one who believes in
> him
> will never be put to shame.

1 Peter 2:6 (CSB)

When my house was inspected for construction flaws, the inspector measured whether the floor was level. Thankfully, it was. A sloping floor would indicate a defective foundation. A building must have a foundation that is aligned and upright. The walls must go straight up. If walls lean, the building will fall eventually.

Jesus is the foundation of the spiritual house God is building—the most important stone. I am a "living stone" in that house. Is my life resting on him? If not, my life will lean too much. My walls will be crooked. My floor won't be level. If my life is founded on Jesus, then the spiritual house will be solid and I will fit together with the other "living stones" in God's house.

PRAYER: Lord, help me to depend on you. Amen.

60 Shame

For it stands in Scripture:

> See, I lay a stone in Zion,
> a chosen and honored corner-
> stone,
> and the one who believes in
> him
> will never be put to shame.

1 Peter 2:6 (CSB)

When I had to write a short professional biography, I wondered whether I should include the fact I belong to a Christian professional society. Would some atheist read it and penalize me? Would my work be criticized, because I'm a Christan? Would I be afraid of identifying as a Christian?

The Scripture reminds me that my hope and trust are in the Lord. He is a solid foundation for all of life, including my professional life. I've never regretted including that Christian professional society in my biography and on my professional Web page.

PRAYER: Lord, I will never be ashamed as long as I stick with you, no matter what the atheist thinks. Amen.

61 Precious

Now to you who believe, this stone is
precious. But to those who do not believe,

> The stone the builders rejected
> has become the cornerstone.

1 Peter 2:7 (NIV)

My wedding ring is precious. Its gold may be valu-
able, but its significance is what makes it precious.
Our rings have a matching fiery design that is special to us. We gave them to each other at our wedding, our special day. My ring represents our precious commitment to each other.

Jesus is precious to me. Because of him, my sins
are forgiven. Because of him, I am a child of God.
Because he committed himself to go to the cross, I
will be faithful to him.

PRAYER: Lord, my relationship with you
is the most precious I have. Amen.

PERSONAL THOUGHTS

62 Atheists

Now to you who believe, this stone is precious. But to those who do not believe,

The stone the builders rejected
has become the cornerstone.

1 Peter 2:7 (NIV)

Some people claim to be atheists. Other just act like it. An atheist has rejected the call to faith. Many atheists don't understand why Christians talk about Jesus so much. "Wasn't he just a good teacher, like Buddha or Muhammad?"

They don't know Jesus rose from the dead and has authority over the universe. He is personally coming back to rule Planet Earth and judge everyone according to what they have done. That could be bad news to those who don't believe. To us who believe in him, this is all good news. We know our sins are forgiven.

PRAYER: Lord, I pray the atheists I know will realize you are there. Amen.

PERSONAL THOUGHTS

63 Stumble

> A stone to stumble over,
> and a rock to trip over.

> They stumble because they disobey the
> word; they were destined for this.
>
> 1 Peter 2:8 (CSB)

I was walking on the sidewalk, minding my own business, when suddenly, I hit the sidewalk face down, hands and knees bleeding. I didn't see the chunk of concrete slab sticking up in my path.

Those who reject the gospel think they are just minding their own business as they go through life. They don't see that rejecting Jesus will cause them to stumble and fall with eternal consequences.

PRAYER: Lord, I pray for my relatives who have rejected you. Amen.

PERSONAL THOUGHTS

64   Royal priesthood

> But you are a chosen race, a royal priest-
> hood, a holy nation, a people for his pos-
> session, so that you may proclaim the
> praises of the one who called you out of
> darkness into his marvelous light.
>
> > 1 Peter 2:9 (CSB)

I had a manager who protected his workers from distractions by the upper management. He would go to boring meetings and write status reports instead of making me write them. He wanted me to be productive and to focus on my regular duties.

God has adopted me through Christ, and made me a member of his royal priesthood. I don't have to go to boring meetings or write status reports. He takes care of anything that would distract me. I am focused on my priestly job of worshiping on behalf of the people of the earth.

PRAYER: Lord, thank you for the privi-
lege of worshiping you. Amen.

PERSONAL THOUGHTS

65   Nation

> But you are a chosen race, a royal priest-
> hood, a holy nation, a people for his pos-
> session, so that you may proclaim the
> praises of the one who called you out of
> darkness into his marvelous light.
>
> 1 Peter 2:9 (CSB)

The "Bulldog Nation" is everyone who has a
connection to the school—students, employees,
alumni, families of students, everyone in town, and
especially football fans. We are loyal to our Bull-
dogs. We cheer for our teams. We tell others what a
great place it is.

In ancient times, *nation* did not imply a polit-
ical state. A nation was an ethnic group with a
shared culture. Now, all believers are God's "holy
nation." Even though we come from many ethnic
backgrounds, we are unified. We are loyal to Jesus
and each other. We rejoice with each other. We tell
others how wonderful life in Christ is.

PRAYER: Lord, thank you for making me
a member of your holy nation. Amen.

PERSONAL THOUGHTS

66   A people

> But you are a chosen race, a royal priest-
> hood, a holy nation, a people for his pos-
> session, so that you may proclaim the
> praises of the one who called you out of
> darkness into his marvelous light.
>
> 1 Peter 2:9 (CSB)

Abraham was chosen to be the ancestor of the Messiah. His family was a chosen people. Their God
was the creator of the universe. Everyone else wor-
shiped idols. Religious Jews in Jesus time thought
they were superior to the all the other nations, because God had chosen Abraham, their ancestor.

Jesus extended the gospel to Gentiles, like me.
He sent his followers to make disciples of all kinds
of people.[20] All believers are God's people, because
of our relationship with him.

> PRAYER: Lord, thank you for making me
> one of your people. Amen.

PERSONAL THOUGHTS

---

[20]Matthew 28:18–20.

67   Special possession

> But you are a chosen race, a royal priest-
> hood, a holy nation, a people for his pos-
> session, so that you may proclaim the
> praises of the one who called you out of
> darkness into his marvelous light.
>
> 1 Peter 2:9 (CSB)

My uncle carved walking canes for a hobby. Each
cane had a gospel story to go with it. He would
take his canes to craft shows and tell the stories to
anyone who came by. I was given one of his canes
as an inheritance. It is a special possession to me. It
reminds me of my uncle's love for Jesus.

The creator of the universe made everything. He
owns it all, but he has picked us to be his special
ones. He made us to be his friends, just like Adam
was in the Garden of Eden.[21] He sent Jesus, so we
can be freed from sin. We are his special possession.

PRAYER: Lord, thank you for making me
special. Amen.

PERSONAL THOUGHTS

---

[21]Genesis 3:8–9.

68 Darkness

> But you are a chosen race, a royal priest-
> hood, a holy nation, a people for his pos-
> session, so that you may proclaim the
> praises of the one who called you out of
> darkness into his marvelous light.
>
> 1 Peter 2:9 (CSB)

The matinee movie had just ended. I was looking
for a way out, but it was dark. Then I saw some
small points of light on the floor. When I followed
the path of those faint lights, I came to a door. When
I opened the door, bright sunshine washed over me.

Living without Jesus in my life is like deep darkness. The gospel pointed me to him. When I believed in him, it was like stepping into bright sunshine. I am thankful that God nudged me along
into his light.

PRAYER: Lord, thank you for a life in
your light. Amen.

PERSONAL THOUGHTS

69 God's people

> Once you were not a people, but now
> you are God's people; you had not re-
> ceived mercy, but now you have re-
> ceived mercy.
>
> 1 Peter 2:10 (CSB)

Almost everybody looked the same at my church in 1983. The only one with dark skin was a man from Jamaica. By 2000, the congregation was about ten times larger and about one fifth African-American, one fifth Hispanic, and the rest mostly white. There were some from Haiti, Finland, and other countries, too. Even though we came from many backgrounds, we were one people in Christ.

Before meeting Jesus, we identified according to our backgrounds. Some of us were just alone, not belonging to any group. But now, God has chosen all who are in Christ to be his people.

> PRAYER: Lord, thank you for putting me among your people. Thank you for uniting us. Amen.

PERSONAL THOUGHTS

70 Mercy

> Once you were not a people, but now
> you are God's people; you had not re-
> ceived mercy, but now you have re-
> ceived mercy.
>
> 1 Peter 2:10 (CSB)

When someone is convicted of a crime, the judge
is responsible for determining the sentence in most
cases. The sentencing phase of the trial brings out
any extenuating circumstances that would affect
the judge's decision. Should it be the maximum or
mercy?

I was a convicted sinner, deserving God's judgment. Before determining my sentence, God considered extenuating circumstances. Namely, Jesus
died on the cross, paying the penalty for my sins,
so that I could receive mercy.

PRAYER: Lord, thank you for granting
mercy to me. Amen.

PERSONAL THOUGHTS

71   Dear friends

> Dear friends, I urge you as strangers and
> exiles to abstain from sinful desires that
> wage war against the soul.
>
> 1 Peter 2:11 (CSB)

I had three business trips to England. On each trip,
I met a different couple who were believers. I visited with them for a few hours and then was on my
way. Over the years, we exchanged Christmas letters. Our friendship bridged the Atlantic.

After about twenty years, my wife and I had a
trip to England. One of the couples hosted us for
the weekend and we reunited with all of them over
tea. Our friendship was fresh and renewed because
we all know the Lord.

The Apostle Peter called me friend even though
we have never met. His greeting has bridged the
centuries, the distance, and cultures. Knowing Jesus is an instant foundation for friendship.

PRAYER: Lord, thank you for friendships
with those who know you. Amen.

PERSONAL THOUGHTS

72 Abstain

> Dear friends, I urge you as strangers and
> exiles to abstain from sinful desires that
> wage war against the soul.
>
> 1 Peter 2:11 (CSB)

At most Mexican restaurants, the first thing on the table is chips and salsa. Angie likes salsa, but if it is too spicy, it does not agree with her stomach later. So after a taste test, she abstains from spicy salsa.

Sinful desires have much worse consequences than spicy salsa. Bad things result when I do whatever I want. My desires are corrupt. That is why Peter implored us to abstain from sinful desires. I want my desires to be molded by what the Lord wants.

PRAYER: Lord, help me abstain from selfish sinful desires. Amen.

PERSONAL THOUGHTS

73   War

> Dear friends, I urge you as strangers and
> exiles to abstain from sinful desires that
> wage war against the soul.
>
> 1 Peter 2:11 (CSB)

My pride was wounded when someone at work
was promoted ahead of me. I sulked for a while.
When I repented of my arrogant ambitious attitude,
the battle with my fleshly desire had been won.

The Word of God warns me to avoid selfish ambition.[22] Such desires are destructive for my soul.
My heavenly Father knows what is best for me. His
plans for me are better than my ambitions. I must
resist arrogance which wars against the person God
intends for me to be.

PRAYER: Lord, help me win the war
against selfish ambition. Amen.

PERSONAL THOUGHTS

---

[22]Philippians 2:3.

74   Among the pagans

> Conduct yourselves honorably among
> the Gentiles, so that when they slander
> you as evildoers, they will observe your
> good works and will glorify God on the
> day he visits.
>
> 1 Peter 2:12 (CSB)

Shortly after I became a Christian, I realized that a
personal relationship with Jesus made me different
than most people around me. As I grew up and
went from one phase of life to the next, the difference became more and more stark.

Even though most Americans say they believe
in God and a majority go to church sometimes, I can
tell they are really pagans. Most worship material-
ism. Some worship other things like sex, sports, the
environment, social justice, or self. So, I live among
the pagans.

> PRAYER: Lord, help me conduct myself
> honorably among the pagans. Amen.

PERSONAL THOUGHTS

75   Slandered

> Conduct yourselves honorably among the Gentiles, so that when they slander you as evildoers, they will observe your good works and will glorify God on the day he visits.
>
> 1 Peter 2:12 (CSB)

When I was working for a government contractor, the time came to write a proposal for the next phase of the job. I was assigned to do some of the writing. Those above me told me to charge the contract on my timecard instead of the overhead account. I refused to do that, because it is illegal. Those around me accused me of being disloyal to the company.

Some accusations come because of standing for righteousness. Other accusations come because I am just nearby. Accusation is the standard way to manipulate others. When I recognize what is going on, I can respond in a godly way instead of just reacting defensively.

> PRAYER: Lord, when conflict comes, show me what is going on beneath the surface. Amen.

PERSONAL THOUGHTS

76   Good works

> Conduct yourselves honorably among
> the Gentiles, so that when they slander
> you as evildoers, they will observe your
> good works and will glorify God on the
> day he visits.
>
> 1 Peter 2:12 (CSB)

My office door was always open. When a student came in, I thought, "Here's another one to
love." Sometimes the student just needed information. Other times, a word of encouragement
was needed. "Yes, you can bring that low grade
up." Occasionally, the student needed advice about
graduate school or a career.

Small kind acts and words are what God expects
me to do. God prepares the way for good works.
They are not hard to do when he is involved.[23]

> PRAYER: Lord, thank you for preparing
> opportunities to do good works. Amen.

PERSONAL THOUGHTS

---

[23]Ephesians 2:10.

77   The day he visits

> Conduct yourselves honorably among the Gentiles, so that when they slander you as evildoers, they will observe your good works and will glorify God on the day he visits.
>
> 1 Peter 2:12 (CSB)

When the favorite uncle came to visit, the kids quit arguing. The accusations that flew yesterday were forgotten. The stories shared with him were about accomplishments, not arguments.

Modern atheists often criticize Christians for their beliefs. "Those ideas are hate-speech!" When Jesus returns to Planet Earth, the accusations of the pagans against Christians will fade away. The pagans will remember the good deeds of believers and tell the Lord all about them.

> PRAYER: Lord, help me do the good you prepared, so you will get the credit. Amen.

PERSONAL THOUGHTS

78 Submit

> Submit to every human authority be-
> cause of the Lord, whether to the em-
> peror as the supreme authority or to
> governors as those sent out by him to
> punish those who do what is evil and to
> praise those who do what is good.
>
> 1 Peter 2:13–14 (CSB)

It is easy to submit to a boss who is knowledge-
able, competent, just, fair, wise, and kind. All of
my working life, I've had a boss, but very few su-
pervisors live up to this ideal.

Jesus wants me to submit to human authority
even when it is not ideal. The authority might be
the boss at work, the policeman on the corner, or
the mayor. The quality of their leadership is not the
issue. I submit for the Lord's sake. By the way, this
will defuse accusations by the pagans that I am disloyal or a rebel.

PRAYER: Lord, help me submit to flawed
authority figures. Amen.

PERSONAL THOUGHTS

79   Emperor

> Submit to every human authority be-
> cause of the Lord, whether to the em-
> peror as the supreme authority or to
> governors as those sent out by him to
> punish those who do what is evil and to
> praise those who do what is good.
>
> 1 Peter 2:13–14 (CSB)

The President of the United States is in the news
every day. Sometimes I like what he has done and
sometimes I don't. I like and respect some presi-
dents personally and some I don't. I'm sure the Roman emperors were worse than any president, yet
Peter said to submit to the emperor.

The Bible teaches me to submit to the authority
of the President whether I like him or not. The Ex-
ecutive branch of our federal government enforces
laws, promulgates regulations, and has many rules.
My job, for the Lord's sake, is to respect and submit
to these rules from the emperor—I mean the President.

> PRAYER: Lord, help me to submit to the
> government's rules out of loyalty to you.
> Amen.

PERSONAL THOUGHTS

80   Governors

> Submit to every human authority be-
> cause of the Lord, whether to the em-
> peror as the supreme authority or to
> governors as those sent out by him to
> punish those who do what is evil and to
> praise those who do what is good.
>
> 1 Peter 2:13–14 (CSB)

Giving exams was one of my duties as a teacher. Then I had to grade them. I had to be honest. Correct answers earn high grades, and some exams earn failing grades.

The Word of God teaches how to handle authority. A good governor rewards the good and punishes the bad. A teacher is in a position of authority, too. So my job was to reward the good and to give poor grades to those who deserved them, namely, those who failed the exams.

PRAYER: Lord, teach me to handle authority properly. Amen.

PERSONAL THOUGHTS

81   Ignorant talk

> For it is God's will that you silence the
> ignorance of foolish people by doing
> good.
>
> 1 Peter 2:15 (CSB)

Worldly people assume I have the same motives as
they do, such as greed, seeking pleasure, and being selfish. But I don't. The gospel gives me other
motives, such as loving enemies, being generous,
and sacrificing self. Godly motives result in good
actions.

Because other people don't know my motives,
they might gossip about me. I don't pay attention
to gossip, so I don't know what they say. They act
surprised when my actions reflect the Jesus way of
living.

PRAYER: Lord, give me your motives in
place of my old worldly motives. Amen.

PERSONAL THOUGHTS

82   Cover-up

> Submit as free people, not using your
> freedom as a cover-up for evil, but as
> God's slaves.
>
> 1 Peter 2:16 (CSB)

There was a big mildew stain on the wall. So I just got some paint to cover it up. After I slopped some paint on the spot, it looked fine. A few weeks later, the stain reappeared. Oh, what a disappointment! That was the wrong way to get rid of a stain. I needed to use the right chemicals and put them on in multiple coats.

My freedom is not the solution to sinful attitudes and desires. Jesus is the one who can remove the stain of sin. If I try to cover up sin, it will become obvious in a little while. My freedom is for glorifying the Lord with good deeds after the sin has been cleaned up.

> PRAYER: Lord, cleanse me from sin in
> my life, so my freedom will glorify you.
> Amen.

PERSONAL THOUGHTS

83   God's slave

> Submit as free people, not using your
> freedom as a cover-up for evil, but as
> God's slaves.
>
> 1 Peter 2:16 (CSB)

Legal slavery was outlawed in America over
150 years ago by the Emancipation Proclamation
and later by the Thirteenth Amendment to the Con-
stitution. But even today, a person may have an
oppressive boss and despair of finding a better job.
With no hope of freedom, he feels like a slave.

Even though I may be legally free, I am willingly
a slave to God. He is never oppressive. He is the
source of abundant living. Even if a human boss is
oppressive, I know my real boss is the Lord. He will
provide a way of escape when the time is right and
strength to endure persecution.

> PRAYER: Lord, I am your slave. Thank
> you for the freedom to serve you. Amen.

PERSONAL THOUGHTS

84 Respect

> Honor everyone. Love the brothers and
> sisters. Fear God. Honor the emperor.
>> 1 Peter 2:17 (CSB)

Everyone likes to be respected by others. Some try to earn respect through professional accomplishments, through sports, or through music. Some take pride in their possessions, such as a home, a muscle car, a collection of things, clothes, or just money. Some expect respect for their family heritage, their job, or social status.

The Lord tells me to honor everyone. The person with a menial job deserves my respect just as much as the accomplished professional. I will respect the drug addict just like the well balanced person. I will respect the unknown mother just as much as the famous pastor.

> PRAYER: Lord, help me to find creative
> ways to honor others. Amen.

PERSONAL THOUGHTS

85   Brothers

> Honor everyone. Love the brothers and
> sisters. Fear God. Honor the emperor.
> 1 Peter 2:17 (CSB)

In high-school History class, I noticed a guy who
spoke up for biblical truth. Even though we went
to different churches, we saw ourselves as brothers,
and we became a tag-team, advocating for God's
principles. Because all believers are in God's family,
we commonly call each other *brother* and *sister*.

Whenever I meet a believer, there is an instant
bond, because we both know Jesus. We can't help
but love each other, because he first loved us.

> PRAYER: Lord, help me recognize and
> love all the fellow believers who cross
> my path. Amen.

PERSONAL THOUGHTS

86 Fear

> Honor everyone. Love the brothers and
> sisters. Fear God. Honor the emperor.
>
> 1 Peter 2:17 (CSB)

I was driving down the Interstate highway. Suddenly, I noticed that the cars in front of me were slowing down. We were getting bunched up well below the speed limit. Then I saw the state trooper with his radar gun. They were afraid of getting a ticket. As soon as I was past the trooper, traffic sped up to five miles per hour over the speed limit.

If I am cautious at the sight of a state trooper's radar gun, how much more cautious should I be when God is watching my life? He sees me all the time. God is the righteous judge who will account for my every thought and action. It is only logical to fear his judgment of sin and to respect his authority to do so.

> PRAYER: Lord, I acknowledge your authority and I know you are the righteous judge. Amen.

PERSONAL THOUGHTS

87 Honor

> Honor everyone. Love the brothers and
> sisters. Fear God. Honor the emperor.
>> 1 Peter 2:17 (CSB)

How would I act if the President of the United
States came to a Bible study at my house? Would
I treat him like any other visitor? Would I demonstrate honor and respect toward him? And how
would I react to his security guards? His en-
tourage? They need the Bible study, too. Sometimes
the person who is elected is not my favorite candi-
date. Sometimes the person who is President does
things I don't like. How would I treat that kind of
person?

The Roman emperors in New Testament times
were not nice guys, not wise rulers, and not friendly
toward Christians. Yet Peter said, "Honor the emperor." God wants me to honor people in authority
irrespective of how they act, what they do, or what
they think about me.

> PRAYER: Lord, if the President comes to
> my house, I will welcome and honor him
> the same as anyone else. Amen.

PERSONAL THOUGHTS

88   Slave

> Household slaves, submit to your mas-
> ters with all reverence not only to the
> good and gentle ones but also to the
> cruel.
>
> 1 Peter 2:18 (CSB)

While representing my department on a committee,
I learned that the vice-president was considering a
new policy that would adversely affect my department. So, I promptly wrote an email about it to
my boss. I didn't want my supervisor to to have
unpleasant surprises. This was my way of demonstrating my loyalty to the business.

Even though modern society does not have slavery like ancient times, nor like the Old South of over
150 years ago, I still have an employer who deserves
my loyalty and submission while I'm on the job.
Seeing myself as a "slave" to my employer helps me
keep a godly attitude throughout the day, in reverent fear of God.

PRAYER: Lord, help me to submit to
my employer with a humble attitude.
Amen.

PERSONAL THOUGHTS

89   Gentle or cruel

> Household slaves, submit to your mas-
> ters with all reverence not only to the
> good and gentle ones but also to the
> cruel.
>
> 1 Peter 2:18 (CSB)

My coworkers and I knew the project was far behind schedule, but the managers kept promising
on-time delivery to the customer. They kept doing
this until the truth could not be hidden anymore. It
is easy to submit when the boss is honest and nice,
but it is hard to keep a submissive attitude when
those above are doing wrong.

Jesus taught me to love my enemies. A cruel
or unethical manager probably qualifies. Love includes submitting and even more. A manager will
be surprised when I give more than was expected
or required. I must mirror the love that Jesus has
for each person, even the unethical manager.

> PRAYER: Lord, help me love others un-
> conditionally, both the gentle and the
> cruel. Amen.

PERSONAL THOUGHTS

90   Enduring injustice

> For it brings favor if, because of a con-
> sciousness of God, someone endures
> grief from suffering unjustly.
>
> 1 Peter 2:19 (CSB)

Sometimes at work, one becomes the victim of un-
fair treatment by others. This is especially difficult
when it happens day after day. Finding another job
may seem impossible. Despair seems like a pit.

The Lord sees my situations. He knows about
injustice. He understands my frustrations. He will
commend me if I will just endure the pain and react
with his grace. What seems impossible with men is
just temporary with God. He provides strength of
character during a trial and a way of escape when
the time is right.

PRAYER: Lord, thank you for giving me
the endurance I need for difficult unjust
situations. Amen.

PERSONAL THOUGHTS

91   Spanked

> For what credit is there if when you do
> wrong and are beaten, you endure it?
> But when you do what is good and suf-
> fer, if you endure it, this brings favor
> with God.
>
> 1 Peter 2:20 (CSB)

When I was little, my mother would spank me or make me sit in a corner, or both. But why did she do this? Either I did something wrong, or I got blamed for something my little sister did. Almost always, Mom knew who the culprit was. She could see what happened when her back was turned.

I didn't get any credit with God for enduring a spanking when it was my fault. But if I get punished for doing good, then enduring it will please the Lord.

PRAYER: Lord, help me have a godly attitude if I am punished unjustly. Amen.

PERSONAL THOUGHTS

92   Christ suffered for you

> For you were called to this, because
> Christ also suffered for you, leaving you
> an example, that you should follow in
> his steps.
>
> 1 Peter 2:21 (CSB)

Crucifixion was a humiliating public spectacle. The condemned was naked. Bystanders taunted. The crosses were set up at a major thoroughfare. His crime was posted on the cross. Jesus was embarrassed for me.

Jesus' trial was a gross miscarriage of justice. The witnesses against him could not agree. Everything he said was true. The governor concluded he was not deserving death. Jesus was executed anyway. He suffered injustice for me.

Jesus bore the sins of the world for all ages. God the Father could not tolerate being with him. Jesus was abandoned for me.

PRAYER: Lord, thank you for suffering for me. Amen.

PERSONAL THOUGHTS

93   Follow

> For you were called to this, because
> Christ also suffered for you, leaving you
> an example, that you should follow in
> his steps.
>
> 1 Peter 2:21 (CSB)

Martin Luther King went to jail for civil disobedi-
ence to protest racist segregation. He was willing to
pay the legal consequences of his protest, because
his actions were based on his Christian convictions.
There are times when a Christian suffers injustice
because he is a Christian.

Jesus suffered injustice. So as a follower of Jesus,
I should not be surprised if I suffer injustice too. My
reaction should be similar to his, because he is my
example. This is something I must resolve in my
heart well before the injustice happens.

PRAYER: Lord, I am willing to follow
your example. Amen.

PERSONAL THOUGHTS

94   Sinless

[Jesus] did not commit sin, and no deceit
was found in his mouth.

1 Peter 2:22 (CSB)

I had casually told a customer about a problem I
was working on. Later, an angry coworker stormed
into my office, accusing me of disloyalty to the company. Yes, I had done what he said, but I didn't feel
disloyal. I didn't know what to say.

When Jesus was on trial, he did not defend himself from injustice with angry words or exagger-
ating the truth. When I am accused, my reaction
should be like Jesus. When I'm in an uncomfortable situation, I should not spin the truth to make
myself look good. In every situation, I must not sin
and must not deceive others.

PRAYER: Lord, help me to avoid deceiving others. Amen.

PERSONAL THOUGHTS

95   Insults

> When [Jesus] was insulted, he did not
> insult in return; when he suffered, he did
> not threaten but entrusted himself to the
> one who judges justly.
>
> 1 Peter 2:23 (CSB)

As the batter stepped to the plate, the fans for the other side were shouting insults at him. "Hey, batter. You're an easy out." They were hoping he would think about the insult he could shout back instead of keeping his eye on the ball.

When Jesus was insulted, he did not retaliate. During his trial he mostly remained silent. He did not threaten to call an army of angels to fight for him. He is my example. How will I react when I am insulted, or when I find out I've been the target of gossip? Will I react like Jesus did?

> PRAYER: Lord, help me to react to insults
> with your grace. Amen.

PERSONAL THOUGHTS

96   Threats

> When [Jesus] was insulted, he did not
> insult in return; when he suffered, he did
> not threaten but entrusted himself to the
> one who judges justly.
>
> 1 Peter 2:23 (CSB)

In the heat of an argument, one little kid might say,
"I'll beat you up!" The other replies "My brother
will beat you up!" and the threats fly back and
forth.

Jesus knew that he could call on twelve legions
of angels to defend himself, but he did not threaten
as he headed toward the cross.[24] Jesus is my example. When I'm not getting my way, I won't threaten
or try to intimidate others. I know God's judgment
is righteous.

PRAYER: Lord, help me refrain from
threating others. Amen.

PERSONAL THOUGHTS

---

[24]Matthew 26:53.

97   Who judges justly

> When [Jesus] was insulted, he did not
> insult in return; when he suffered, he did
> not threaten but entrusted himself to the
> one who judges justly.
>
> 1 Peter 2:23 (CSB)

There are many courts in America. Family court, ju-
venile court, bankruptcy court, traffic court, county
court, state court, federal court, appeals court, and
the Supreme Court are all part of the system. Even
if every court corrupts justice, there remains a
higher court, higher than the Supreme Court. God
is the righteous judge who will judge what every
person has done.

  The trial of Jesus was a great miscarriage of justice. He was completely innocent. He did not
protest or argue to protect himself. He knew that
God the Father judges righteously, and he would
set things right in the end. If I suffer injustice, I
know the righteous judge will vindicate me, too.

PRAYER: Lord, thank you for your righteous judgments. Amen.

PERSONAL THOUGHTS

98   He bore our sins

> [Jesus] himself bore our sins in his body
> on the tree; so that, having died to sins,
> we might live for righteousness. By his
> wounds you have been healed.
>
> 1 Peter 2:24 (CSB)

The furniture arrived in several big cardboard boxes. We cut them open and unpacked everything. We looked around and felt like we were drowning in cardboard scraps. Then our neighbor's son volunteered, "I'll take the cardboard away in my pickup." So we loaded up the cardboard and he bore our mess away.

Jesus bore all of my sin when he went to the cross. Life can look like a sea of cardboard scraps. Sin is overwhelming, but Jesus bore my mess away. Now, I am clean and can live for righteousness.

PRAYER: Lord, thank you for carrying my mess away. Amen.

PERSONAL THOUGHTS

99   Weeds

> [Jesus] himself bore our sins in his body
> on the tree; so that, having died to sins,
> we might live for righteousness. By his
> wounds you have been healed.
>
> 1 Peter 2:24 (CSB)

Sand spurs were everywhere in my yard. I wanted them all to die, but I wanted the grass to live. Sand spurs are hard to kill; they are unaffected by most weed killers. Even if you pull up the weed, the seeds are left behind to sprout when you aren't looking.

Without the cross of Jesus, sin sprouts up like a weed. Therapy to pull out one kind of sin doesn't prevent the seeds from sprouting sin all over again. But Jesus bore our sins, so that I am no longer compelled to sin.

> PRAYER: Lord, thank you for freeing me
> to live righteously. Amen.

PERSONAL THOUGHTS

100   Healed

> [Jesus] himself bore our sins in his body
> on the tree; so that, having died to sins,
> we might live for righteousness. By his
> wounds you have been healed.
>
> 1 Peter 2:24 (CSB)

Everyone gets sick from time to time. Sometimes my God-designed immune system fights an infection. I appreciate the God-given wisdom of doctors. Sometimes the Holy Spirit tells me how to change my lifestyle for the better. Sometimes God miraculously heals.

I know the God who heals. I'm not shy to pray for healing for anyone against any disease. I'm thankful for healing no matter which mechanism the Lord uses. Sin is a "disease" that needs an eternal solution. Jesus died, so that I can be healed from sin and disease.

PRAYER: Lord, thank you for healing me
from sin and disease. Amen.

PERSONAL THOUGHTS

101   Astray

> For you were like sheep going astray, but
> you have now returned to the Shepherd
> and Overseer of your souls.
>
>   1 Peter 2:25 (CSB)

After exploring the Noxubee Wildlife Refuge, it was
time to head for home. Instead of going home the
way we came, I decided to try out our new GPS
unit,[25] "Jill." I pushed the buttons and off we went.
Down the road, Jill said, "Turn right." I looked
right and saw a dirt logging road, just a couple of
ruts through the woods. So we stayed on the paved
road. Jill said "Recalculating." In a few minutes, Jill
said, "Turn right." Another dirt logging road with a
pair of overgrown ruts. This happened a few more
times and eventually the paved road took us to the
highway more than 10 miles out of our way.

If I follow the world's advice instead of the Word
of God, I'll end up on a bumpy overgrown trail
in the middle of nowhere. If I follow my selfish
inclinations, I'll wander around, straying from the
Lord's destiny for me, but if I follow Jesus and obey
his teaching, I will never be led astray.

> PRAYER: Lord, help me follow your
> guidance, so I don't go astray. Amen.

---

[25]Global Positioning System (GPS).

102 Shepherd

For you were like sheep going astray, but you have now returned to the Shepherd and Overseer of your souls.

1 Peter 2:25 (CSB)

Psalm 23, "The Lord is my shepherd," was in the program at the funeral. Someone read the psalm aloud during the service. The psalm reminded me of how Grandma had lived close to God. She was an inspiration to me. I miss her and her love deeply. How can I get along without her?

Psalm 23 reminds me that I can't lean on a human shepherd. "The Lord is my shepherd." I must return to the "Shepherd and Overseer" of my soul well before my own funeral.

PRAYER: Lord, you are my shepherd. Amen.

PERSONAL THOUGHTS

103   Won without words

In the same way, wives, submit your-
selves to your own husbands so that,
even if some disobey the word, they
may be won over without a word by the
way their wives live when they observe
your pure, reverent lives.

1 Peter 3:1–2 (CSB)

Everyone experiences difficult relationships. I had
an unbelieving roommate who did a variety of
things that, as a Christian, I could not participate
in. I had to maintain a roommate relationship while
living as a follower of Jesus. That meant doing
helpful things and declining some of his invitations
without being judgmental.

Peter advised submitting in such difficult relationships while living pure, reverent lives. There
may be good spiritual fruit later. Someone watching may be won without words.

PRAYER: Lord, help me be pure and reverent in the middle of my difficult relationships. Amen.

PERSONAL THOUGHTS

104   Rumpled

> Don't let your beauty consist of out-
> ward things like elaborate hairstyles and
> wearing gold jewelry or fine clothes, but
> rather what is inside the heart—the im-
> perishable quality of a gentle and quiet
> spirit, which is of great worth in God's
> sight.
>
> 1 Peter 3:3–4 (CSB)

My wife says I was rumpled when we got married.
I was working at a corporate office at the time. The
executives believed in "dress for success." My beat-
up boots weren't professional looking. Eventually,
I realized that if I wore a suit everyday, the executives would listen to my advice, so I wore a suit to
please them. My wife has helped me become less
rumpled.

Hair styles, jewelry, and clothes are works of
art that convey a message. Peter said true beauty
comes from within. My external art should convey
the internal reality, a gentle and quiet spirit, which
looks beautiful to God.

PRAYER: Lord, help me exhibit beauty of
the heart. Amen.

PERSONAL THOUGHTS

105   Uncluttered

> For in the past, the holy women who put
> their hope in God also adorned them-
> selves in this way, submitting to their
> own husbands.
>
> 1 Peter 3:5 (CSB)

My wife and I have been trying to maintain a quiet
gentle lifestyle. This means we give away things we
don't need and decorate sparingly. The uncluttered
decor looks peaceful, not busy.

The women of faith in the Old Testament are
good examples for me. They put their hope in God.
They received promises from God along with their
husbands. Their beauty came from gentle spirits
and their personalities. I want an uncluttered internal life like the women of old who had gentle
personalities, and by the way, I won't accumulate
clutter in the house.

PRAYER: Lord, help me maintain an uncluttered life. Amen.

PERSONAL THOUGHTS

106   Not intimidated

> For in the past, the holy women who put
> their hope in God also adorned them-
> selves in this way, submitting to their
> own husbands, just as Sarah obeyed
> Abraham, calling him lord. You have
> become her children when you do what
> is good and do not fear any intimida-
> tion.
>
> 1 Peter 3:5–6 (CSB)

When I was just beginning my career, I was in a
routine business meeting. Someone proposed an
unethical business practice. Even though I was supposed to just listen, I challenged the unethical idea.
I wondered if I would lose my job.

Sarah was completely submitted to her husband,
Abraham. Even though husbands in her culture
had total authority over the family, Sarah had confidence, because she did what was right for her husband and her household.

Like Sarah, I knew that if I did the right thing,
God would take care of me. By the way, I did not
lose my job.

> PRAYER: Lord, thank you for confidence
> in the face of intimidation. Amen.

107   Understanding

> Husbands, in the same way, live with your wives in an understanding way, as with a weaker partner, showing them honor as coheirs of the grace of life, so that your prayers will not be hindered.
>
> 1 Peter 3:7 (CSB)

I worked at the computer help desk as part of my job. "Hello, what are the symptoms of your problem?...Press that key again...What does it say in the corner?..." One evening, my wife seemed to be having trouble with the computer, so I immediately put on my help-desk hat and started asking questions and making suggestions.

She said, "Let me figure this out for myself!"

I did not understand her wishes. Peter said I should understand and honor her wishes. I've been learning to respect her and think before I speak and act.

PRAYER: Lord, help me be an understanding husband. Amen.

PERSONAL THOUGHTS

108   Dead zone

> Husbands, in the same way, live with your wives in an understanding way, as with a weaker partner, showing them honor as coheirs of the grace of life, so that your prayers will not be hindered.
>
> 1 Peter 3:7 (CSB)

When I sat in my easy chair, my cell phone would not work. I didn't have any "bars." If I went to the dining room window, I barely had enough signal from the cell tower to make a call. We lived in a cell-phone dead zone.

Prayer is like a phone call. If I don't respect my wife as a coheir of the kingdom of heaven, and if I am not considerate and kind toward her, then I will be living in a prayer dead zone. I certainly don't want that. I need the power of God working in answered prayer.

> PRAYER: Lord, help me to find creative ways to honor my wife, so my prayers will be effective. Amen.

PERSONAL THOUGHTS

109   Like-minded

Finally, all of you be like-minded and sympathetic, love one another, and be compassionate and humble.

1 Peter 3:8 (CSB)

Some high schools have a Debate Club where students learn to argue with each other. Some of those students grow up to be lawyers or theologians. Some people have the life-long hobby of arguing about opinions with everyone.

Be like-minded means I should not be argumentative. Opinions just don't matter very much, but the truth of the Bible lasts forever. My opinions are not more important than my place in the community of faith. Putting the Word of God into practice is more important than precisely interpreting every nuance.

PRAYER: Lord, teach me to be less argumentative. Amen.

PERSONAL THOUGHTS

110 Sympathetic

Finally, all of you be like-minded and
sympathetic, love one another, and be
compassionate and humble.

1 Peter 3:8 (CSB)

I carefully tuned the strings of my guitar. When I
played a note on one string that was the same note
as another string, the second string started to sing,
too. This is called *sympathetic vibration.*

If my heart is tuned the same as yours, then I
will rejoice when you rejoice and mourn when you
mourn.[26] If my heart is in tune with yours, we will
have a harmonious relationship. When I tune my
heart to the Word of God, then I am ready to feel
your hurts and joys.

PRAYER: Lord, help me be more sympathetic with others. Amen.

PERSONAL THOUGHTS

---

[26]Romans 12:15.

111   Love one another

> Finally, all of you be like-minded and sympathetic, love one another, and be compassionate and humble.
>
> 1 Peter 3:8 (CSB)

Brotherly love starts by being born into the same family. It is strengthened by spending time together and shared experiences. It is expressed in generosity. It shines in the middle of crisis. Brotherly love is based on relationship.

Christians are born again into God's family. We are brothers and sisters in Christ. We share the experience of knowing Christ through the Holy Spirit. We share experiences in the context of the local church. Brotherly love in Christ is based on relationships.

> PRAYER: Lord, help me love my Christian brothers and sisters more deeply. Amen.

PERSONAL THOUGHTS

112   Compassionate

> Finally, all of you be like-minded and
> sympathetic, love one another, and be
> compassionate and humble.
>
> 1 Peter 3:8 (CSB)

Joan and her husband cooked a big pot of soup on Saturdays from time to time. They loaded it into the car, drove to the park, and fed the homeless. The open trunk was like the kitchen table. Their compassion for people was demonstrated by acts of kindness.

I want to be more like Joan. I want to be compassionate toward others like she was. When I think about how God has been compassionate toward me, I feel more compassion toward others.

> PRAYER: Lord, your compassion toward
> me has been overwhelming. Help me
> be more compassionate toward others.
> Amen.

PERSONAL THOUGHTS

113   Humble

> Finally, all of you be like-minded and sympathetic, love one another, and be compassionate and humble.
>
> 1 Peter 3:8 (CSB)

The Queen of England is at the pinnacle of the social order. Everyone in her domain gives her honor and many people around the world do, too. Her humility shines when she honors a commoner.

Because God loves me, I am adopted into his royal family. I am high class in Christ. Because God loves you, you are royalty and high class, so I honor you above myself.

Humility is obvious when it is counter to worldly social conventions. The world looks down on the poor and on low social class. Humility shines when I honor someone unexpectedly.

> PRAYER: Lord, show me opportunities to honor someone who does not expect it. Amen.

PERSONAL THOUGHTS

114   Repay

> Not paying back evil for evil or insult
> for insult but, on the contrary, giving a
> blessing, since you were called for this,
> so that you may inherit a blessing.
>
> 1 Peter 3:9 (CSB)

If I borrow something, I must repay the loan with the same stuff. If I borrow ten dollars, I can't repay with apples.

Revenge works the same way. If I am wounded, revenge means I want to wound my enemy the same way. That's the way the world works.

The Jesus way is different. I must repay evil with blessing. Jesus said, "Love your enemies,"[27] namely, those who hate me. Revenge is not an option for me, but I still have to repay the ten dollars.

PRAYER: Lord, help me pray for blessing
on those who hurt me. Amen.

PERSONAL THOUGHTS

---

[27]Matthew 5:43–44.

115 Lies

> For the one who wants to love life
> and to see good days,
> let him keep his tongue from evil
> and his lips from speaking deceit.
>
> 1 Peter 3:10 (CSB)

You: "Hey Ed! How are you ?"

Me: "Fine." But I have a sinus headache and it feels like my head will explode. I am a liar.

You: "Hey Ed! Where have you been?"

Me: "Shopping."

You: "What did you buy?"

Me: "Oh, some stuff for a project." But I just bought a birthday present for you. I am a deceiver.

Modern society accepts "white lies" as morally okay. Politically correct speech calls black white and white black. In English class, kids are taught to eschew obfuscation, but adults obscure the truth and deceive one another.

> PRAYER: Lord, let me always speak truthfully and live openly and honestly. Amen.

PERSONAL THOUGHTS

116   Do good

> For the one who wants to love life
> and to see good days...
> and let him turn away from evil
> and do what is good.
>
> 1 Peter 3:10–11 (CSB)

Willie Sutton, a famous bank robber, was asked why he robbed banks. He replied, "That's where the money is." The world has long recognized that the easiest way to "get rich quick" is to take it from someone else.

The world assumes that money can buy happiness and being rich means a "good life." Some rob banks, others cheat their customers, and others (figuratively) stab coworkers in the back to get ahead.

However, the rich often have more problems than ordinary folks. Those who rob banks usually go to jail. The Lord is the one who gives a good life to those who repent and do good.

> PRAYER: Lord, instead of walking toward evil, I will walk toward the good. Amen.

PERSONAL THOUGHTS

117   Seek peace

> For the one who wants to love life
> and to see good days...
> Let him seek peace and pursue it.
>   1 Peter 3:10–11 (CSB)

Visitors to our house often say, "It's so peaceful here." I've wondered what makes our house different. Knickknacks and photos are not vying for attention on every square inch of wall space. We generally don't have the TV on. My wife and I work at maintaining peace in our relationship, and to let physical things reflect the inner peace we have in the Lord.

God's peace is much more than the absence of conflict. It includes an attitude that doesn't worry about sin, that is confident in God's provision, and that seeks opportunities to be kind to others.

PRAYER: Lord, help me to live in your peace. Amen.

PERSONAL THOUGHTS

118   Attentive

The eyes of the Lord are on the righteous
and his ears are open to their prayer.
But the face of the Lord is against
those who do what is evil.

1 Peter 3:12 (CSB)

When I was little, my Mom and Dad paid attention to what my sister and I were doing. They made sure we didn't do anything dangerous, and if I fell and skinned my knee, they heard my screams.

My heavenly Father is interested in what I am doing, what I am thinking, and where I am going. He warns me when danger is ahead. He listens when I cry out. He comforts me when my tears overwhelm me. He answers my requests.

PRAYER: Lord, thank you for paying attention to me. Amen.

PERSONAL THOUGHTS

119 Against

> The eyes of the Lord are on the righteous
> and his ears are open to their prayer.
> But the face of the Lord is against
> those who do what is evil.
>
> 1 Peter 3:12 (CSB)

My team's football game is this weekend. We're feeling pretty good, because we're on a winning streak. Never mind that those teams weren't very good. This weekend we're facing the Number One team in the country. Guess who will win.

Those who do evil think they're on a winning streak. Never mind that they were facing mere men. Now, justice is coming and they are facing the maker of the universe. He is against those who do evil. Guess who will win.

PRAYER: Lord, you are the almighty creator of the universe. Amen.

PERSONAL THOUGHTS

120   Devoted to good

> Who then will harm you if you are de-
> voted to what is good?
>
> 1 Peter 3:13 (CSB)

Angie volunteered to teach English to internation-
als, mostly wives of university students. Angie's
class was sponsored by the local Baptist churches.
It was an opportunity to show Christ's love to others from around the world. We developed many
precious friendships through the connections that
began in her class.

There are hundreds of opportunities in the
community to volunteer and contribute something
good. No one complains if I do something good for
others, especially for those I don't know.

> PRAYER: Lord, show me the opportuni-
> ties for good you want me to do. Amen.

PERSONAL THOUGHTS

121   Suffering for righteousness

> But even if you should suffer for righ-
> teousness, you are blessed. Do not fear
> what they fear or be intimidated, but in
> your hearts regard Christ the Lord as
> holy.
>
> 1 Peter 3:14–15 (CSB)

Sometimes someone will complain if my good work
interferes with their sin. A small business or professional career can be ruined by an avalanche of Internet complaints. It seems anything done in public
associated with Christ might be subject to an expen-
sive lawsuit, such as prayer at a public meeting, a
statue in the park, or a billboard at the edge of town.

But the Word of God says, "You are blessed. Do
not fear!" Some inconvenience, expense, worry, and
other suffering may be involved, but those things
are insignificant compared to the favor of God.

PRAYER: Lord, I won't be intimidated to
neglect righteousness. Amen.

PERSONAL THOUGHTS

122   Lord

> But even if you should suffer for righ-
> teousness, you are blessed. Do not fear
> what they fear or be intimidated, but in
> your hearts regard Christ the Lord as
> holy.
>
> 1 Peter 3:14–15 (CSB)

In ancient times, *lord* meant the relationship be-
tween a king and a subject, or a master and a slave.
Kings and masters had absolute authority. Amer-
icans don't recognize anyone's absolute authority.
That is what the rebellion in 1776 was all about.
Then slavery was abolished about 150 years ago.
The word *lord* doesn't mean much to most of us.

But now, as a believer, I submit to Jesus as my
absolute ruler. He is the master; I am the slave.
Even though he does not call me a slave, in my
heart I regard him has my lord.

> PRAYER: Lord, because you are the cre-
> ator of the universe and my savior from
> sin, I acknowledge you as my lord.
> Amen.

PERSONAL THOUGHTS

123   Defense

> [Be] ready at any time to give a defense
> to anyone who asks you for a reason for
> the hope that is in you.
>
> 1 Peter 3:15 (CSB)

In the college dorm, we would debate philosophy and religion late into the night. My roommates and friends down the hall were mostly atheists. Sometimes a Jew would join the debate. I quickly learned to be ready for their challenges.

My personal experiences were much more persuasive than debate points or abstract theology. There were times when an intellectual issue was an honest stumbling block, but more often the intellectual sparring was a diversion to avoid confronting the gospel and the reality of the resurrected Christ.

> PRAYER: Lord, prepare me to give your
> answers to any who ask me why I trust
> in you. Amen.

PERSONAL THOUGHTS

124   Gentleness

> [Be] ready at any time to give a defense to anyone who asks you for a reason for the hope that is in you. Yet do this with gentleness and respect.
>
> 1 Peter 3:15–16 (CSB)

If someone asks why I'm happy today, how should I answer? Should I think, "Here's a prospective convert!" An aggressive attitude to convince someone to believe in Jesus just doesn't work. Criticizing a person's lifestyle before they believe doesn't work. Treating someone like a prize in an evangelism game doesn't work.

When I am asked about my faith, a gentle answer earns respect. Treating each person as thoughtful, intelligent, and beloved by God is what the Lord wants from me.

> PRAYER: Lord, help me to always respond to people with gentleness and respect. Amen.

PERSONAL THOUGHTS

125   Conscience

> Keeping a clear conscience, so that when
> you are accused, those who disparage
> your good conduct in Christ will be put
> to shame.
>
> 1 Peter 3:16 (CSB)

When I'm working on a project, sawdust flies everywhere, wood scraps fall on the floor, and paint drips onto the workbench and the floor. My wife walks in and says, "What a mess!" I look around. All my tools are put away and I think, "This looks pretty nice and neat."

Someone's conscience can be corrupted by habits, rationalizations, and just lying to oneself. When I yield to the Holy Spirit, he shows me areas that I thought were nice and neat, but are really a mess. Repentance and perseverance clear away the debris for a truly clear conscience.

> PRAYER: Lord, show me the debris in my
> life that needs to go. Amen.

PERSONAL THOUGHTS

126   Accused

> Keeping a clear conscience, so that when
> you are accused, those who disparage
> your good conduct in Christ will be put
> to shame.
>
>   1 Peter 3:16 (CSB)

Angie was doing her best to mentor some younger
ladies in the faith. One of them became angry with
her and started accusing her to others at church.
Angie was called to the Associate Pastor's office to
answer the slander. After some discussion, the situation was resolved.

Accusations can be subtle, like gossip or jokes,
or they can be aggressive or even public, like a lawsuit. I can't always prevent slander, but a clear conscience means that when the truth comes out, I'll be
exonerated.

> PRAYER: Lord, help me keep a clear con-
> science, even when accused. Amen.

PERSONAL THOUGHTS

127 Suffering for good

> For it is better to suffer for doing good, if
> that should be God's will, than for doing
> evil.
>
> 1 Peter 3:17 (CSB)

The government's justice system is supposed to penalize criminals for doing evil. Sometimes they
come after someone doing good, calling good evil.
The police, the IRS, the EPA,[28] or a homeowners' as-
sociation, any of them, can misbehave. Sometimes
trolls on the Internet can gang up on someone to
ruin a career or a small business.

Because Jesus suffered unjustly, it is not surprising when the world unjustly attacks a Christian for
doing good.

> PRAYER: Lord, I won't be surprised
> when the world attacks me for doing
> good. Amen.

PERSONAL THOUGHTS

---

[28]Government agencies include the Internal Revenue Service (IRS) and the Environmental Protection Agency (EPA).

128   Christ suffered

> For Christ also suffered for sins once for
> all, the righteous for the unrighteous,
> that he might bring you to God. He was
> put to death in the flesh but made alive
> by the Spirit.
>
> 1 Peter 3:18 (CSB)

When I was ten years old, I went to a Christian
camp. During a camp chapel service, I found out
that my trying to be good was not enough to please
God. I knew that I had sinned ever since I was little.
I found out that Jesus suffered the penalty for me,
but was resurrected from the dead. So I asked God
for forgiveness and invited him into my life. I felt
like a big burden had been lifted off of me.

Jesus died on the cross a criminal's death even
though he only did good. Jesus bore my penalty so
that I can be a child of God instead of his enemy. Jesus was righteous. I was unrighteous. He suffered
for me.

PRAYER: Lord, thank you for forgiving
my sin. Amen.

PERSONAL THOUGHTS

129 About face

> For Christ also suffered for sins once for
> all, the righteous for the unrighteous,
> that he might bring you to God. He was
> put to death in the flesh but made alive
> by the Spirit.[29]
>
> 1 Peter 3:18 (CSB)

When I was a Boy Scout, I learned how to do an "about face" when marching. I would take a step with my right foot and then quickly pivot, so I ended up going in the opposite direction.

Jesus rose from the dead. This was the pivot event of human history, moving from death to life. Jesus did it by God's power. His resurrected body was different from before but recognizable. He could go through locked doors, but the nail prints were in his hands. He could eat broiled fish and break bread with his hands.

Because he rose from the dead, I have hope for resurrection by his power and hope for eternal life. The Holy Spirit in me reassures me that this is not an empty hope. Eternal life began when I asked him into my life.

PRAYER: Lord, thank you for eternal life. Amen.

---

[29]Bible scholars disagree radically about the meaning of 1 Peter 3:19–20, so we will skip these verses. Blum, "1 Peter," p. 241.

130   Resurrection power

> Baptism, which corresponds to this, now saves you (not as the removal of dirt from the body, but the pledge of a good conscience toward God) through the resurrection of Jesus Christ.
>
> 1 Peter 3:21 (CSB)

I was about twelve years old when I was baptized in water. Following the traditional method of my church, I went under the water and then rose up. I had decided for myself to take this step. It represented that I was serious about following Jesus and doing what he says.

The water of baptism symbolizes resurrection. Resurrection means leaving death behind to live in new life, a life with a clear conscience, because God forgave my sin. The resurrection of Jesus is the guarantee that bodily resurrection awaits us, but I have a clear conscience now. It takes resurrection power to live the kingdom-of-God lifestyle, which I can do now.

PRAYER: Lord, thank you for the power to live with a clear conscience. Amen.

PERSONAL THOUGHTS

131 Over angels, authorities, and powers

> [Jesus Christ] has gone into heaven and
> is at the right hand of God with angels,
> authorities, and powers subject to him.
>
> 1 Peter 3:22 (CSB)

Jesus ascended to heaven after his resurrection. He
is over "angels, authorities, and powers." Obviously, angels are submitted to God, but most human authorities and demons are in rebellion. Jesus
is the king whether they like it or not.

While Jesus was on earth, he demonstrated his
power over demons by casting them out of people
who were demonized. When Jesus returns, he will
require the allegiance of human authorities. At the
last judgment, the demons will get what they deserve.

> PRAYER: Lord, I'm glad angels, authori-
> ties, and demons will be subject to you
> in the end. Amen.

PERSONAL THOUGHTS

132   Pain

> Therefore, since Christ suffered in the
> flesh, arm yourselves also with the same
> understanding—because the one who
> suffers in the flesh is finished with sin.
>
> 1 Peter 4:1 (CSB)

Nobody likes pain. In America, most physical pain
is due to medical problems, but there are areas
of the world today where people are persecuted,
beaten, jailed, tortured, and executed for being a
Christian.

Jesus was willing to suffer excruciating pain for
me, even to the point of death. Martyrs for the faith
feel the pain like Jesus. They know that suffering
for the faith is more important than any other concern in life. When one is so focused on the eternal,
sin is not tempting any more.

> PRAYER: Lord, I am resolved to focus on
> the eternal whether I am persecuted or
> not. Amen.

PERSONAL THOUGHTS

133   Do the important things

In order to live the remaining time in the
flesh no longer for human desires, but
for God's will.

1 Peter 4:2 (CSB)

I have a to-do list. It seems as long as my arm. Every day I'm confronted with the question, "What is the highest priority today?" The highest priority item may not be the most fun.

One of my favorite slogans is "Do the important things before the urgent things." The trick is knowing what is important.

Selfish human priorities fade in importance compared to doing the will of God. Suffering for the gospel gives a person new priorities, living for the will of God rather than for human desires.

PRAYER: Lord, I will put following your will above my selfish priorities. Amen.

PERSONAL THOUGHTS

134   Party

> For there has already been enough time
> spent in doing what the Gentiles choose
> to do: carrying on in unrestrained be-
> havior, evil desires, drunkenness, orgies,
> carousing, and lawless idolatry.
>
> 1 Peter 4:3 (CSB)

I went to a party with some coworkers. They were
worldly folks. I should have known that their idea
of a "good party" was getting drunk, getting high,
coarse jokes, and sexual immorality. Unfortunately,
I was stuck for the evening, because I didn't have a
car.

Worldly parties are filled with sin to cover up
the emptiness inside. My idea of a good party is
when I can show brotherly love to others, have encouraging conversations, and let the joy of the Lord
flow.

PRAYER: Lord, thank you for your joy
that can enliven any party. Amen.

PERSONAL THOUGHTS

135   Not going to the party

> [The pagans] are surprised that you
> don't join them in the same flood of wild
> living—and they slander you.
>
> 1 Peter 4:4 (CSB)

After getting stuck a few times at parties I wanted
to leave, I just declined to go with the guys. They
didn't understand why a worldly drunken party
was not fun for me.

Sometimes the Christian life means not joining
the crowd around me. I don't always fit in. For a
Christian, *normal* is not a holier-than-thou attitude.
The normal Christian life is being kind to others
and having joy in clean fun without relying on in-
toxicants to feel good.

> PRAYER: Lord, I like your definition of a
> normal life. Amen.

PERSONAL THOUGHTS

136   Who judges everyone

> [The pagans] will give an account to the
> one who stands ready to judge the living
> and the dead.
>
> 1 Peter 4:5 (CSB)

When I was called for jury duty, the judge explained the charges against the defendant. The jury selection process made sure no one was biased or had a conflict of interest. The attorneys were ready to present the evidence.

When Jesus returns he will be the unbiased judge. He will judge impartially. Every person will give an account for what he has done. The evidence will be presented. Those living at the time and those who have died throughout the centuries will stand before him. Sin will be judged.

I'm thankful that Jesus paid the penalty for my sins. I have received God's forgiveness, so I can face the final judgment without fear.

> PRAYER: Lord, thank you for forgiving
> my sinful conduct. Amen.

PERSONAL THOUGHTS

137   Martyrs

> For this reason the gospel was also
> preached to those who are now dead, so
> that, although they might be judged in
> the flesh according to human standards,
> they might live in the spirit according to
> God's standards.
>
> 1 Peter 4:6 (CSB)

In 2015, the Islamic State executed a group of
Egyptian Coptic Christians who were working in
Libya.[30] They never expected to be martyrs for the
faith. They were just doing their jobs to support
their families. But then they were judged by the Islamic State's evil human standards.

They will be resurrected to life on the Last Day.
The Lord will say, "Well done," according to his
standards.

> PRAYER: Lord, I want to be faithful to the
> end like these martyrs. Amen.

PERSONAL THOUGHTS

---

[30]"2015 kidnapping and beheading of Copts in Libya,"
Wikipedia. Available at https://en.wikipedia.org/wiki/2015_
kidnapping_and_beheading_of_Copts_in_Libya (Current June
20, 2019).

138 Are we there yet?

> The end of all things is near; therefore,
> be alert and sober-minded for prayer.
>> 1 Peter 4:7 (CSB)

When my sister and I were small, we took family trips. Like most kids, we said, "Are we there yet?" We were eager to get there. We wanted to play with cousins. We wanted to hug Grandma's neck. We were hungry. We had a thousand and one reasons. "Are we there yet?"

I'm eager for Jesus to return. I want to visit with the saints who have gone before us. I want to tell Jesus I love him to his face. I am hungry to see the kingdom of heaven on earth. I have a thousand and one reasons. "Come, Lord Jesus!"[31]

PRAYER: Lord, I am eager to see you. Amen.

PERSONAL THOUGHTS

---

[31]Revelation 22:20.

139   Serious

The end of all things is near; therefore,
be alert and sober-minded for prayer.
1 Peter 4:7 (CSB)

Final exams were coming next week. I knew I had
to study more. I had to stay alert. Maybe coffee
would help. No distractions were allowed. The situation was serious. Maybe prayer would help.

Jesus is coming soon. The world is a mess and
is not getting better. I'm keeping aware of current
events. Stay calm. Don't overreact to the next crisis.
The situation is serious. Prayer is the only thing left
to do.

PRAYER: Lord, come soon, because this
world is a mess. You are the only one
who can clean it up. Amen.

PERSONAL THOUGHTS

140 Constant love

> Above all, maintain constant love for
> one another, since love covers a multi-
> tude of sins.
>
> 1 Peter 4:8 (CSB)

When I was a kid, our house had an artesian well
for watering the grass. Water flowed without needing a pump. Sometimes we kids cooled off by
splashing in the water. My love for others is like
water from a deep well that will never run dry.
The power of the Holy Spirit sustains my love so
it never fails.

Constant love means forgiving, covering sin.
The Lord has forgiven me, so I must forgive others. Forgiveness opens the door for me to love the
offender. I will respond to others with forgiveness
and love no matter how much they sin against me,
loving constantly.

> PRAYER: Lord, help me to constantly
> love and forgive my fellow believers.
> Amen.

PERSONAL THOUGHTS

141   Love covers

> Above all, maintain constant love for one another, since love covers a multitude of sins.
>
> 1 Peter 4:8 (CSB)

When I went camping, sometime I refilled my canteen with some clean fresh water from a stream. As long as I did not stir up the bottom, the water would remain clear. If I touched the bottom, a cloud of sediment would cloud the stream and I could not use it.

When I forgive someone, I'm not allowed to think about it anymore. It is covered. Unforgiveness and bitterness stir up old offenses, clouding life and making it unpotable, but love covers old sins.

PRAYER: Lord, help me avoid thinking about old forgiven offenses. Amen.

PERSONAL THOUGHTS

142   Hospitality

> Be hospitable to one another without complaining.
>
> 1 Peter 4:9 (CSB)

I was over 1,200 miles from home. Thanksgiving holiday was coming and I had no place to go. It felt pretty lonely. Then a fellow Christian student, who was also far from home, invited me to go with him to Thanksgiving dinner at his uncle's home nearby. There were about ten people around the table from several countries. The conversation around the table was interesting. The occasion filled a hole in my life.

I'm very thankful for the hospitality I've received from believers all over the world. It is comforting to know I have family among believers. In turn, I try to be hospitable toward others.

PRAYER: Lord, help me recognize opportunities to be hospitable. Amen.

PERSONAL THOUGHTS

143   Serving

> Just as each one has received a gift, use it
> to serve others, as good stewards of the
> varied grace of God.
>
> 1 Peter 4:10 (CSB)

Joan had the ability to talk to anyone about Jesus in
the natural course of conversation. It never seemed
like she was trying to recruit proselytes. There was
no hint of any ulterior motive. She just had that
ability.

Everyone has natural talents and abilities. All
of them are gifts from God. Some are public in nature and some are exercised in private. Some are
rare and some are widespread. Some are artistic
and some are practical craftsmanship. Some are re-
lational and some are personal.

Whatever my abilities may be, I should use
them to benefit others. Selfishness never yields last-
ing benefits. God did not give me my talents and
abilities to gain fame and fortune. He gave them so
I can serve others.

> PRAYER: Lord, help me find creative
> ways to serve others. Amen.

PERSONAL THOUGHTS

144   Speak God's words

> If anyone speaks, let it be as one who
> speaks God's words; if anyone serves,
> let it be from the strength God provides,
> so that God may be glorified through Je-
> sus Christ in everything. To him be the
> glory and the power forever and ever.
> Amen.
>
> 1 Peter 4:11 (CSB)

The phone rang. A friend was upset. There was a
crisis in her family. Angie encouraged her, gave her
some common-sense biblical advice, and prayed
with her.

Speaking God's words doesn't just happen in
church. The words don't sound religious, but they
hit the heart. They give life. Every time I open
my mouth, I want God's words to come out, in everyday conversation and in crisis, in church and in
the grocery store, a trail of life-giving words everywhere I go.

PRAYER: Lord, help me to speak your
words in every situation of life. Amen.

PERSONAL THOUGHTS

145   God's strength

If anyone speaks, let it be as one who speaks God's words; if anyone serves, let it be from the strength God provides, so that God may be glorified through Jesus Christ in everything. To him be the glory and the power forever and ever. Amen.

1 Peter 4:11 (CSB)

The small church could not afford to hire a janitor. So each Thursday, Angie and a couple of other ladies vacuumed all the carpet in the church. Then it was ready for Sunday. They served the Lord with the strength he provided.

Service to others is an expression of our worship to God. Believers who serve never become famous, even though they are faithful year after year, but the Lord notices. He supplies the stamina to get the job done, and will reward their faithfulness.

PRAYER: Lord, I want to serve others for no other reason but worship of you. Thank you for your strength. Amen.

PERSONAL THOUGHTS

146   Glory and power

> If anyone speaks, let it be as one who
> speaks God's words; if anyone serves,
> let it be from the strength God provides,
> so that God may be glorified through Je-
> sus Christ in everything. To him be the
> glory and the power forever and ever.
> Amen.
>
> 1 Peter 4:11 (CSB)

When a spokesman makes an announcement for a
company, who gets credit for the announcement?
The spokesman does not. The president of the company does. When an employee gets paid to work at
a charity event, who gets thanked? The boss who
sent the employee does.

Jesus gets the credit when I speak the words he
gives me. Jesus gets the credit when I serve with
the strength he gives. Those who understand my
source will praise God.

PRAYER: Lord, you deserve all the glory
and power. Amen.

PERSONAL THOUGHTS

147   Fiery ordeal

> Dear friends, don't be surprised when
> the fiery ordeal comes among you to test
> you as if something unusual were hap-
> pening to you.
>
> 1 Peter 4:12 (CSB)

Ranchers in central Florida from time to time burn
the underbrush on their land so the grass will grow.
The fire clears away the thickets of palmetto. Some
of the pine trees are burned, but most are just
scarred. The ashes of the fire fertilize the ground.
The heat of the fire opens the pine cones so that
seedling pine trees will get started. The fiery ordeal
of the pine-studded pasture is actually beneficial.

In Peter's time, Christians were sometimes persecuted by the Roman government.   Today, in
some parts of the world, Christians are persecuted
severely. Even in America, some Christians are persecuted for standing up for what is right.   Like
the fire in the pine-studded pasture, a fiery ordeal
makes the gospel grow, it opens up hard-hearted
people, and clears away unproductive underbrush
in my life.

> PRAYER: Lord, when a severe test of
> faith comes, help me see the benefits.
> Amen.

148   Not surprised

> Dear friends, don't be surprised when
> the fiery ordeal comes among you to test
> you as if something unusual were hap-
> pening to you.
>
> 1 Peter 4:12 (CSB)

When the founding pastor retired, a thriving church
hired a new pastor. Before long, the new pastor's ef-
forts to cultivate deeper spiritual life had offended
about half the congregation and some of the elders.
Some left and some stayed. Even after several years,
the animosity and division remained fresh. The experience felt like a fiery ordeal.

Jesus had enemies. The religious establishment
conspired to execute him. The Roman government
didn't care about justice.

It is not surprising that believers have enemies,
too. Sometimes it is the religious establishment.
Sometimes it is the government, a homeowners' as-
sociation, or a civic club. Sometimes it is the media or Internet trolls. Sometimes it is coworkers,
friends, or even family. The very existence of a righteous life exposes sin. Those entangled in sin don't
like that. Some will be drawn to the gospel and
some will reject it.

> PRAYER: Lord, I won't be surprised
> when I encounter an enemy of the
> gospel. Amen.

149 Suffering for Christ

> Instead, rejoice as you share in the suf-
> ferings of Christ, so that you may also
> rejoice with great joy when his glory is
> revealed.
>
> 1 Peter 4:13 (CSB)

On Easter, 2019, the teacher of a Sunday School class at Zion Church in Batticaloa, Sri Lanka, asked "How many of you are willing to die for Christ?"[32] All of the children raised their hands. Each one signified fresh dedication to Jesus by lighting a candle. After Sunday School, they went to the church's main service. They passed through an outside courtyard where a stranger was speaking with some church leaders. Suddenly, there was an explosion. Half the children died on the spot. Twenty-six people died and about a hundred were injured by the suicide bomber. For those children who died, lighting that candle was their final act of worship.

These victims were true martyrs for the faith. They will be overjoyed when resurrected on the day Jesus returns to earth.

> PRAYER: Lord, give me the courage to be
> willing to die for you. Amen.

---

[32]Jayson Casper, "Sri Lankan Sunday School Was 'Willing to Die for Christ' on Easter. Half Did," *Christianity Today*, April 25, 2019. https://www.christianitytoday.com/news/2019/april/sri-lanka-easter-isis-zion-sunday-school-sebastian-funerals.html (Current June 20, 2019).

150   The big reveal

> Instead, rejoice as you share in the sufferings of Christ, so that you may also rejoice with great joy when his glory is revealed.
>
> 1 Peter 4:13 (CSB)

When the Oscars are awarded by the Academy of Motion Pictures, no one in the audience knows which movie will be Best Picture. At the big moment, the winner is revealed. Those of us who had seen the movies may have thought we knew which was best, but the "big reveal" had to wait until awards night.

When Jesus returns to earth, everyone will know that he is the rightful king of the universe. His glory as king will be revealed to all. Right now, Christians know by faith who Jesus is. We won't be a surprised. We will rejoice to see him fulfill his reign and to see our faith validated.

> PRAYER: Lord, I will be overjoyed when your reign is revealed to everyone. Amen.

PERSONAL THOUGHTS

151 Ridiculed

> If you are ridiculed for the name of
> Christ, you are blessed, because the
> Spirit of glory and of God rests on you.
>
> 1 Peter 4:14 (CSB)

Christians in America are being insulted more and
more for principles the Bible clearly teaches. If a
Christian publicly challenges the latest atheist pro-
gressive narrative, then he is likely to be ridiculed
in the media and on the Internet. Even wearing a
t-shirt with a Christian message invites an attack.

The victim of insults is actually blessed because
God's glory rests on that person. I feel so blessed as
a child of God that I don't notice ridicule for being
a Christian.

> PRAYER: Lord, let your Spirit rest on me,
> especially if I'm ridiculed. Amen.

PERSONAL THOUGHTS

152   Meddler

> Let none of you suffer as a murderer, a
> thief, an evildoer, or a meddler.
>
> 1 Peter 4:15 (CSB)

Nobody likes a meddler. A meddler is likely to be insulted, to lose friends, and to become an outcast.

Meddlers are grouped with murderers, thieves, and other criminals. Meddling is sin in God's eyes, even though it is not punished by society like crimes. Pride is the root of meddling. "I know how to run your life better than you do." The truth is I don't. Moreover, each person is responsible for his own life and his own actions. The meddler does not have that responsibility.

If I'm going to stick my nose in someone else's business, I'd better be sure my advice is welcome.

PRAYER: Lord, show me the difference between being helpful and meddling. Amen.

PERSONAL THOUGHTS

153   Having that name

> But if anyone suffers as a Christian, let
> him not be ashamed but let him glorify
> God in having that name.
>
> 1 Peter 4:16 (CSB)

In the first century, *Christian* was a derogatory la-
bel. Roman writers called Christians *atheists*, because they would not worship the wide variety of
gods in their society.

In modern society, people claim to be atheists,
but chase after a host of gods, such as wealth, success, drugs, sports, and hobbies. Some people claim
to be Christians, but chase after those same things.
They might go to church with Mom on Christmas,
Easter, and Mother's Day.

I want my life to show that I follow Jesus. I'm
not chasing those other things. I don't mind if it's
obvious I'm a believer, even though I don't preach
about it.

PRAYER: Lord, let my life glorify you because I'm a believer. Amen.

PERSONAL THOUGHTS

154   Judgment

> For the time has come for judgment to
> begin with God's household, and if it
> begins with us, what will the outcome
> be for those who disobey the gospel of
> God?
>
> 1 Peter 4:17 (CSB)

I've heard many Christians say, "I used to get away
with such and such, but now that I'm a Christian, I
get caught every time." Even if a sin is not illegal,
it will backfire on the Christian. An unbeliever can
do the same thing and seem successful.

The Bible teaches that each person is responsible for his own sin. God will discipline his children
before judgment falls on unbelievers. God loves us
too much to let us stay in our sinful patterns.

PRAYER: Lord, correct me when I fall into
a sinful pattern. Amen.

PERSONAL THOUGHTS

155 Saved

> And if a righteous person is saved with difficulty, what will become of the ungodly and the sinner?
>
> 1 Peter 4:18 (CSB)

I thought I was doing fine, until my wife said, "You always do what you want anyway." She had exposed my selfishness. I had to repent. Growing spiritually always has bumps along the way.

Even though a believer is saved in eternity by the righteousness of Christ, actions still have consequences. Those who live right most of the time are still responsible for their own sins.

The ungodly and the unbeliever are stuck in patterns of sin. If God disciplines believers, then God's judgment will surely fall on the ungodly.

PRAYER: Lord, help me to do right all the time. Amen.

PERSONAL THOUGHTS

156 Suffering

> So then, let those who suffer according to God's will entrust themselves to a faithful Creator while doing what is good.
>
> 1 Peter 4:19 (CSB)

In 2014, an elderly man who regularly fed the homeless from a pot of soup in the trunk of his car was arrested.[33] The city of Fort Lauderdale, Florida, commanded him to stop, because he did not have a permit to be a restaurant and his kitchen had not been inspected accordingly. Controversy over the city's actions continued.

Sometimes doing a good deed gets criticized or even penalized. Being a Good Samaritan[34] is often not commended or rewarded. How should a believer respond to such criticism? Keep on doing good.

PRAYER: Lord, Help me to be persistent in spite of criticism. Amen.

[33]Chris Spargo, "Florida charity worker, 90, arrested by police for feeding the homeless gets right gets arrested again one day later," *Daily Mail*, November 5, 2014. Available at https://www.dailymail.co.uk/news/article-2822829/Charity-worker-90-arrested-police-feeding-homeless-gets-right-work-one-day-later-despite-outcry-insensitive-mayor-gets-arrested-again.html (Current June 20, 2019).

[34]Luke 10:30–37.

157   Elders

> I exhort the elders among you as a fel-
> low elder and witness to the sufferings
> of Christ, as well as one who shares in
> the glory about to be revealed:
>
>   1 Peter 5:1 (CSB)

Over the years, I've attended churches governed
in various ways: bishops, pastors, deacons, elders,
councils, and so on. When the leaders were mature
humble disciples of Jesus, things went well. The
formalities didn't seem to matter much. I appreciate all the leaders who have had a hand in my spiritual growth.

In ancient Israel, through New Testament times,
the most senior man in an extended family was an
elder in the village. The apostles appointed elders
in each new urban church to govern that community. Personal qualities were the criteria for ap-
pointing elders rather than extended family relationships.[35]

Church leaders have a difficult job helping us
mature. Many of us come into a church as spiritual
babies, so our actions are often not Christ-like. I
pray for my church's leaders often, because I know
they need strength and wisdom from the Lord to
cope with the rest of us.

> PRAYER: Lord, thank you for the mature
> leaders you have placed in my churches.
> Amen.

---

[35]1 Timothy 5:17–21 and Titus 1:5–9.

158 Witness

> I exhort the elders among you as a fellow elder and witness to the sufferings of Christ, as well as one who shares in the glory about to be revealed:
>
> 1 Peter 5:1 (CSB)

In court, a witness has credibility when he explains what he personally saw. The judge and the jury want to know the truth about the situation. Peter was an eye witness of Jesus' crucifixion and also his resurrection.

I can be an indirect witness about Jesus' sufferings to my friends. The gospels tell me what happened the day Jesus died. They also tell me about the resurrection a few days later. Tradition says the gospel of Mark was based on Peter's teaching. Matthew and John were eye witnesses like Peter. Luke carefully researched the material in his gospel. I know the truth indirectly, because I know the gospel writers were reliable witnesses.

PRAYER: Lord, help me be a better witness to my friends. Amen.

PERSONAL THOUGHTS

159   Glory revealed

> I exhort the elders among you as a fellow elder and witness to the sufferings of Christ, as well as one who shares in the glory about to be revealed:
>
> 1 Peter 5:1 (CSB)

When I finished a test at school, I didn't know whether I made an A. I may have thought so, but I wasn't sure. When the graded test came back to me, it revealed whether I got an A or not.

Christians embrace the gospel by faith. Is Jesus really the Messiah? Is he really the Son of God? A believer who is persecuted for the gospel must be pretty sure, but there is still the element of faith.

When Jesus returns to Planet Earth, "every eye will see"[36] and "every knee will bow"[37] in worship. When the glory of Jesus is revealed, believers will know their faith is true. Jesus will give every believer an A.

> PRAYER: Lord, I am eager to see your glory revealed. Amen.

PERSONAL THOUGHTS

---

[36]Revelation 1:7.
[37]Philippians 2:10.

160   Shepherd God's flock

Shepherd God's flock among you, not
overseeing out of compulsion but willingly, as God would have you; not out
of greed for money but eagerly.

1 Peter 5:2 (CSB)

I have been a member or co-leader of small home
Bible studies for most of my life. Over and over,
I have seen many spiritually good things happen
when leaders love the members.

Leaders of small groups function like shepherds
(pastors), but they are not the pastor of a local congregation. Group leaders also are like sheep dogs.
Sheep dogs protect the sheep and run after strays
to guide them back to the flock. That is what group
leaders do.

PRAYER: Lord, thank you for the leaders
of small groups who helped me grow in
the faith. Amen.

PERSONAL THOUGHTS

161   Willing

> Shepherd God's flock among you, not
> overseeing out of compulsion but will-
> ingly, as God would have you; not out
> of greed for money but eagerly.
>
> 1 Peter 5:2 (CSB)

Our small home Bible study had grown too large, so we recruited new leaders from among the members to lead two smaller new groups. The week before the new groups were to start, one of the new leaders dropped out of sight and would not answer the phone. We had misjudged his willingness to love the sheep.

Pastors, elders, and small group leaders must love the people under their care. Love cannot be legislated or mandatory. It must be voluntary. Therefore leaders in the church must be willing and have pure motives.

> PRAYER: Lord, I thank you for the lead-
> ers who willingly give of themselves.
> Amen.

PERSONAL THOUGHTS

162   Not for the money

> Shepherd God's flock among you, not overseeing out of compulsion but willingly, as God would have you; not out of greed for money but eagerly.
>
> 1 Peter 5:2 (CSB)

Over the years, I've observed how various churches and ministries manage their finances. Peter advised church leaders not to be motivated by financial gain. Modern supporters of a church or ministry expect a high standard of openness and honesty with regard to finances.

A leader's extravagant lifestyle smells like greed, even when the money was gained honestly. Christian leaders should be good examples of honesty, good financial management, generosity, and a modest lifestyle.

Constant appeals for donations smell like greed. Christian people should be taught to give where the Holy Spirit directs, instead of just responding to an emotional appeal. Ministries should look to the Lord to supply needs. Answers often do come through donations.

> PRAYER: Lord, help me to hear the Holy Spirit regarding where and how much to give. Amen.

163   Not lording over them

> Not lording it over those entrusted to you, but being examples to the flock.
>
> 1 Peter 5:3 (CSB)

Parents always want the best for their children, even when the children are adults. Little kids need direction and boundaries. Some parents find it difficult to let go as their kids mature, and still give intrusive direction when the kids are grown.

Some Christian leaders feel like parents toward the flock. So they feel they must give direction whether it is needed or not. Peter explained that spiritual leadership is by example, not by direction. Directions may result in outward obedience or rebellion, but the Lord wants the flock to have righteousness from the heart.

PRAYER: Lord, help me be a good example to other believers. Amen.

PERSONAL THOUGHTS

164   Crowns

> And when the chief Shepherd appears,
> you will receive the unfading crown of
> glory.
>
> 1 Peter 5:4 (CSB)

While our friends were on vacation, we took care of their calico cat. The cat made sure we knew it was time for an early breakfast even on Saturdays. When our friends returned, they gave us a thank-you gift.

Jesus identified himself as the Good Shepherd.[38] His parables explained how he cares for his sheep. When Jesus returns, he will reward leaders who have cared for his flock. Thank-you gifts among friends are small things, but the reward from Jesus to those who care for his flock will be glorious.

PRAYER: Lord, help me do my part to care for your flock. Amen.

PERSONAL THOUGHTS

---

[38]John 10:11,14.

165   Submitted to elders

> In the same way, you who are younger,
> be subject to the elders.   All of you
> clothe yourselves with humility toward
> one another, because
>
>> God resists the proud
>> but gives grace to the humble.
>
> 1 Peter 5:5 (CSB)

Ever since I became a Christian, there have been many godly people who were older than me who have helped me mature: a Sunday School teacher, a youth leader, some graduate students when I was a freshman, many pastors and church elders, home Bible study leaders, and others. I am thankful for their examples and for their concern for me.

Peter taught younger believers to submit to the elders of the local congregation. They have experiences in the faith that will help younger believers grow.

> PRAYER: Lord, now that I am older, help me be a worthy example to the younger generation. Amen.

PERSONAL THOUGHTS

166   Humility

> In the same way, you who are younger,
> be subject to the elders.   All of you
> clothe yourselves with humility toward
> one another, because
>
>> God resists the proud
>> but gives grace to the humble.
>
> 1 Peter 5:5 (CSB)

Our culture has a variety of customs to show honor to others. Commons courtesies include holding a door open for someone else, letting someone into traffic safely, saying "please," "thank you," and "you're welcome," and expressing sympathy when someone experiences tragedy.

Humility is about honoring others above myself. Humility is a decision. *Clothing myself* means I will make honoring others a routine part of life. I will honor you above myself.

> PRAYER: Lord, help me see creative ways to honor others. Amen.

PERSONAL THOUGHTS

167   Opposition

> In the same way, you who are younger,
> be subject to the elders.   All of you
> clothe yourselves with humility toward
> one another, because
>
> > God resists the proud
> > but gives grace to the humble.
>
> > 1 Peter 5:5 (CSB)

The job of a bouncer is to keep unruly patrons out
of a nightclub and let well behaved patrons in. A
bouncer is typically a lot bigger than most people.
Like a bouncer who opposes the unruly, the Lord
"resists the proud."

The proud will want to take control and get
things done "for the Lord."   The Lord doesn't
need that kind of help. The proud will want the
credit and congratulations for their accomplishments. The Lord doesn't share his glory. The proud
will want to be paid for any expenses. The Lord
loves a cheerful giver. Whatever the proud tries to
accomplish, the Lord opposes. The proud feel en-
titled to God's best, but he gives his favor to the
humble instead.

> PRAYER: Lord, I will cultivate humility
> so you won't resist me. Amen.

168   Exalted

> Humble yourselves, therefore, under the mighty hand of God, so that he may exalt you at the proper time.
>
> 1 Peter 5:6 (CSB)

One of my coworkers wanted to be a programmer but did not have a college degree. She took a job as a computer operator and studied programming on the side. The department manager gave her some programming tasks. Over time, she demonstrated her programming skill. Eventually, she was promoted to a programmer job.

In God's kingdom, worldly skills, money, and social status don't count. A humble heart is what the Lord is looking for. If I will humble myself, God will promote me to roles and responsibilities. He will provide the direction, skills, and resources for whatever he asks me to do.

PRAYER: Lord, help me to consistently humble myself. Amen.

PERSONAL THOUGHTS

169   Anxiety

Casting all your cares on him, because he cares about you.

1 Peter 5:7 (CSB)

I shared a house with three other guys. The landlady let us know she was going to sell the house and we had to move in a month. We all agreed to move together to some other house. We were anxious about finding a suitable place. In faith, I told the guys to be ready to move out on the third Saturday and we would clean the old place on the fourth Saturday. God provided a place for us a few days before the third Saturday.

Difficult situations happen all the time. How will I react? Will anxiety take over? Or will faith take over?

PRAYER: Lord, thank you for your care for me. I'll try to quit worrying. Amen.

PERSONAL THOUGHTS

170   The devil

> Be sober-minded, be alert. Your adversary the devil is prowling around like a roaring lion, looking for anyone he can devour.
>
> 1 Peter 5:8 (CSB)

Popular culture portrays the devil as the ruler of hell with red skin, horns, and a pitchfork. The Bible tells us the devil is a real spiritual being, but he is not the master of hell's fire. Hell, described in Revelation as a lake of fire, will be designed to torment the devil and his demons at the end of the age.[39]

The devil wants to victimize people, but Jesus has defeated the devil. Jesus cast out demons and rose from the dead. We defeat the devil's deception by proclaiming God's truth.

> PRAYER: Lord, help me to recognize the devil's schemes and to respond in faith. Amen.

PERSONAL THOUGHTS

---

[39]Revelation 20:10.

171   Resist

> Resist [the devil], firm in the faith, know-
> ing that the same kind of sufferings are
> being experienced by your fellow believ-
> ers throughout the world.
>
> 1 Peter 5:9 (CSB)

When we read reports from Christians around the
world, we see that fellow believers are often tar-
geted victims of the devil's evil ways. The devil
works through people and organizations to wreak
havoc on the innocent. Our struggle is not with
people, but with the spiritual power for evil that
influences people.[40]

Whenever I'm faced with demonic oppression,
my strategy is to be firm in faith, resisting the evil. I
know the Lord is more powerful than anything the
devil can do. The Lord may give the victory now, or
on the Last Day. I may be exonerated or martyred.
I will stand in faith.

PRAYER: Lord, give me your strength to
resist the devil and his allies. Amen.

PERSONAL THOUGHTS

---

[40]Ephesians 6:12.

172   God's grace

> The God of all grace, who called you to
> his eternal glory in Christ, will himself
> restore, establish, strengthen, and sup-
> port you after you have suffered a little
> while.
>
> 1 Peter 5:10 (CSB)

The grace of God is like a coin; it has two sides. He
does not give me the death I deserve and he gives
me abundant life I don't deserve. Like everyone
else, I've sinned plenty of times. My selfishness results in sinful thoughts and actions. I'm forgiven,
because Jesus died and rose from the dead.

As a believer, I've welcomed God into my life. I
see the work of the Holy Spirit inside. I have righteousness, peace, and joy[41] due to the grace of God.
Living with God's grace is much better than living
without it.

PRAYER: Lord, thank you for your grace.
Amen.

PERSONAL THOUGHTS

---

[41]Romans 14:17.

173   Eternal glory

> The God of all grace, who called you to his eternal glory in Christ, will himself restore, establish, strengthen, and support you after you have suffered a little while.
>
> 1 Peter 5:10 (CSB)

Sometimes a friend will say, "I once shook hands with Mr. So-and-so." Because Mr. So-and-so is a movie star, politician, or sports star, contact with him lets a bit of his fame rub off in a handshake. Sometimes a fan refuses to wash the hand that touched a rock star. Of course, fame and glory are not contagious.

In Christ, my destiny is eternal glory. The glory will not be due to anything I have done, not because I deserve anything, but rather because God's grace allows me to hang around with Jesus. When Jesus returns, his glory will be obvious. Believers will be with him and will reflect his glory.

> PRAYER: Lord, help me function like a mirror where people see your glory instead of me. Amen.

PERSONAL THOUGHTS

174   Strengthened

> The God of all grace, who called you to
> his eternal glory in Christ, will himself
> restore, establish, strengthen, and sup-
> port you after you have suffered a little
> while.
>
> 1 Peter 5:10 (CSB)

I was fighting a cold. I was sneezing and coughing.
My nose was running. It was uncomfortable and
inconvenient, but it was not significant compared
to the trials and pains some others experience.

Life has its ups and downs. Christians are not
exempt from the normal trials of life. Some believers suffer because of loyalty to Jesus.

No matter how severe the downs of life, the
Lord has promised to bring me through. I will be
stronger, established, and restored in my faith after
I have seen the unlimited power of God working on
my behalf.

PRAYER: Lord, thank you for working
on my behalf. Amen.

PERSONAL THOUGHTS

175   Dominion

To him be dominion forever. Amen.
1 Peter 5:11 (CSB)

This brief verse is a doxology which sounds to me like a fragment of a song. Perhaps Peter's readers knew the rest of the song. He only had to quote one line to bring it to mind. I like to sing about how the Lord reigns, too.

God will rule his creation forever. I acknowledge his authority and power. He rules with justice and righteousness.

> PRAYER: Lord, I praise you for your righteous reign over all creation. Amen.

PERSONAL THOUGHTS

176   Faithful brothers

> Through Silvanus, a faithful brother (as
> I consider him), I have written to you
> briefly in order to encourage you and to
> testify that this is the true grace of God.
> Stand firm in it!
>
> 1 Peter 5:12 (CSB)

When I was single, I shared a house with some fellow believers. During a snow storm, a brother's car
slid into a snow bank and got stuck about a mile
from home. The next day we worked together to
dig the car out of the snow. Cooking together and
cleaning house together built bonds among us, too.

There were seasons where we prayed together
at 6:00 am before the first one left for work. They
were short but precious prayer times.   Faithful
brothers share life, both practical things and spiritual things.

PRAYER: Lord, thank you for the faithful
brothers you have put in my life. Amen.

PERSONAL THOUGHTS

177   True grace

> Through Silvanus, a faithful brother (as I consider him), I have written to you briefly in order to encourage you and to testify that this is the true grace of God. Stand firm in it!
>
> 1 Peter 5:12 (CSB)

Peter knew his letter stated the truth, because he had lived it. He had walked with Jesus. He had felt and seen the power of the Holy Spirit. He had experienced forgiveness. He knew the grace of the gospel is true. Because it is true, his letter is full of encouragement.

Even though skeptics may argue, I have experienced the same grace as Peter in my Christian walk. I've felt the same encouragement. I've seen the same power of the Holy Spirit. I know the gospel of Jesus is true grace.

PRAYER: Lord, thank you for the true grace of the gospel. Amen.

PERSONAL THOUGHTS

178 Greetings from far away

> She who is in Babylon, chosen together
> with you, sends you greetings, as does
> Mark, my son.
>
> 1 Peter 5:13 (CSB)

When my wife and I visited China, we were es-
corted to an underground house-church meeting.
There were about twenty people in an apartment
living room. We shared how our church in Florida
was praying for them. They were surprised and
touched to know that fellow Christians half way
around the world were concerned for them.

The love of Jesus reaches around the world
among Christians. Greetings from far away are encouraging, especially for those who are surrounded
by unbelievers.

> PRAYER: Lord, I intercede for the believ-
> ers I know who are scattered around the
> world. Amen.

PERSONAL THOUGHTS

179   Greet one another

Greet one another with a kiss of love.
Peace to all of you who are in Christ.
1 Peter 5:14 (CSB)

When I greet my sister's family, there is an instant
bond, because we are family. She and I had growing up years together. Her husband is one of my
best friends with many shared times. I've watched
my nieces and nephew grow up. These shared experiences bind us together in love. When we say
goodbye, we pray for peace and safe travel.

We Christians have an instant bond because we
all know Jesus. When we meet, a heart-felt affec-
tionate greeting is natural. When we say goodbye,
we pray for peace and safe travel.

PRAYER: Lord, give peace and safe travel
to each believer I encounter. Amen.

PERSONAL THOUGHTS

Meditations on 2 Peter

180   Servant

> [Simon] Peter, a servant and an apostle
> of Jesus Christ: To those who have re-
> ceived a faith equal to ours through the
> righteousness of our God and Savior Je-
> sus Christ.
>
> 2 Peter 1:1 (CSB)

When I was inducted into the Army, I became completely committed to defend my country. The Army
could assign me to any job they wanted. I was obli-
gated to obey my commanders. I felt like a slave.

Peter considered himself as a slave to Jesus.
Even though he was in the inner circle of Jesus'
friends, Peter saw himself as a servant. He had
completely submitted his life to Jesus.

In ancient times, slaves were bought and sold.
My life has been purchased by the blood of Jesus.
I have submitted my life to Jesus. I want to obey
every directive Jesus gives me.

PRAYER: Lord, help me be a faithful servant to you. Amen.

181   Equal faith

> [Simon] Peter, a servant and an apostle of Jesus Christ: To those who have received a faith equal to ours through the righteousness of our God and Savior Jesus Christ.
>
> 2 Peter 1:1 (CSB)

I have faith that the chair I'm sitting in will hold me up. You have faith that the same chair will hold you up, too. If the Apostle Peter were here, he would have the same faith in the same chair.

Peter and the other apostles had great faith. Peter said my faith in the Lord is similar to his. A new believer's faith is the same as the Apostle Peter's. A child's faith is the same as an adult's. The faith of an American is the same as a Chinese person, even though they live on opposite sides of Planet Earth.

Christians do not have various kinds of faith. One person's faith is not better than someone else's faith. Jesus' righteousness is the reason all Christians have similar faith. The Lord gives the gift of faith to all who are willing. His mercy cleanses us from sin.

PRAYER: Lord, thank you for the gift of faith. Amen.

182 Favor

> May grace and peace be multiplied to you through the knowledge of God and of Jesus our Lord.
>
> 2 Peter 1:2 (CSB)

As I was grading a student's last programming homework assignment of the semester, I noticed that his friend's name was embedded in the program. The student had been so desperate that he just copied his friend's homework. His grades were already very low, and this was a pathetic attempt to keep from sinking further. I decided to give him the minimum punishment allowed, and coach him about academic honesty. I gave him favor.

Grace is God's favor. Because of his favor, I received forgiveness for my sins. Because of his favor, I have peace in my soul. Because of his favor, I have fellowship with him. I have grace in abundance, because God is generous. Knowing the Lord Jesus is why I have access to the heavenly Father's generosity.

PRAYER: Lord, thank you for your generosity. Amen.

PERSONAL THOUGHTS

183   Peace

> May grace and peace be multiplied to
> you through the knowledge of God and
> of Jesus our Lord.
>
> 2 Peter 1:2 (CSB)

The lagoon looked like glass in the early morning
sun. A few hundred yards from shore, a patch of
ripples said a puff of breeze was making its way
across the water, pushing a sailboat on its way.

The peace of God in my life is like the glassy lagoon. The breath of the Holy Spirit is like that puff
of breeze, going wherever it wants. I don't have
to be concerned by the chaos and confusion of the
world around me. I have the peace of God within.

The Holy Spirit makes ripples on my heart when
correction is needed. He powers my sails when I
need to move to appointments he has set for me.

> PRAYER: Lord, thank you for the peace
> of the Holy Spirit in my heart. Amen.

PERSONAL THOUGHTS

184   Power

[God's] divine power has given us everything required for life and godliness through the knowledge of him who
called us by his own glory and goodness.

2 Peter 1:3 (CSB)

My car's engine uses gasoline to turn the wheels
and take me where I need to go. The gasoline that's
squirted into the engine's cylinders explodes to provide the power.

God's power explodes within me, so I can live a
godly life for him. I don't need any supplements
or additives. He is sufficient. He knows what I
need for everyday life, and he supplies the moral
strength to reject sin.

PRAYER: Lord, thank you for the ability
to live for you. Amen.

PERSONAL THOUGHTS

185   Knowing him

> [God's] divine power has given us ev-
> erything required for life and godli-
> ness through the knowledge of him who
> called us by his own glory and good-
> ness.
>
> 2 Peter 1:3 (CSB)

Every few weeks, I take my car to the gas station
to fill my gas tank. Then when I need power to go
down the road or up a hill, it is available.

Knowing Jesus fills my spiritual "gas tank." The
Bible reveals Jesus in action and in his teaching, but
I get to know him personally when the Holy Spirit
speaks directly to me. The Holy Spirit has spoken
to me most clearly while I'm studying the Bible.
Sometimes the words jump off the page and I know
the verse is for me to apply. The Lord gives me
his power "for life and godliness" through knowing him.

PRAYER: Lord, thank you for revealing
yourself to me. Amen.

PERSONAL THOUGHTS

186   Called

> [God's] divine power has given us ev-
> erything required for life and godli-
> ness through the knowledge of him who
> called us by his own glory and good-
> ness.
>
> 2 Peter 1:3 (CSB)

When kids are at a playground, one might call to
another, "Come over here to play some soccer!"
The prospect of a good time attracts more and more
friends to the game.

God wants everyone to repent and be saved, but
the natural man is such a sinner that he doesn't seek
God for freedom from sin. So God has revealed
his glory and goodness to appeal to mankind. His
glory is so spectacular that we want to see more.
His goodness is so wonderful that we want to be
with him and be like him. His glory and goodness are calling so that whoever will repent will be
saved.

PRAYER: Lord, I'm glad I responded to
your glory and goodness. Amen.

PERSONAL THOUGHTS

187   Keeping promises

> By these [God] has given us very great
> and precious promises, so that through
> them you may share in the divine na-
> ture, escaping the corruption that is in
> the world because of evil desire.
>
> 2 Peter 1:4 (CSB)

Scientists estimate that the universe began about
13.8 billion years ago. My lifespan of "threescore
and ten"[42] or a few more is only a speck compared
to the universe's age. The age of the universe is only
a speck compared to eternity.

Eternal life is the most important of God's
promises to me. Unlike we humans, God always
keeps his promises. I try my best to keep my
promises and vows, but sometimes I promise the
impossible. Sometimes I don't have the will power
to follow through. Sometimes circumstances intervene. But God always keeps his promises, even for
eternity.

PRAYER: Lord, thank you for always
keeping your promises. Amen.

PERSONAL THOUGHTS

---

[42]Psalm 90:10 (KJV).

188   Promises

> By these [God] has given us very great
> and precious promises, so that through
> them you may share in the divine na-
> ture, escaping the corruption that is in
> the world because of evil desire.
>
> 2 Peter 1:4 (CSB)

When I borrow money from a bank or use a credit
card, I am promising to pay it back. People generally try to fulfill their promises, but sometimes they
are not able or stubbornly refuse.

God has promised wonderful quality of life for
those who trust him. He promised the Holy Spirit
will live in me. He promised to prepare good works
for me to do. He promised to provide what I need.
He promised peace in my inner man. He promised
to give me love for those around me, even the ob-
noxious ones, and even those who hate me. He has
promised joy that will flow out of my soul irrespective of the circumstances around me. It all adds up
to a quality of life that the world can never achieve.

PRAYER: Lord, thank you for giving me
your quality of life. Amen.

PERSONAL THOUGHTS

189 Divine nature

> By these [God] has given us very great
> and precious promises, so that through
> them you may share in the divine na-
> ture, escaping the corruption that is in
> the world because of evil desire.
>
> 2 Peter 1:4 (CSB)

A butterfly is a familiar symbol of being "born
again."[43] A caterpillar has one nature. It feasts on
leaves. It crawls around. A caterpillar builds a cocoon. When freed from the cocoon, the butterfly
emerges. It has a different nature. It feeds on nec-
tar. It flies from flower to flower.

I am a new creature in Christ.[44] The Holy Spirit
in me has given me new desires, new insight, and
new perspective. I am intent on living as a citizen
of the kingdom of heaven should.

> PRAYER: Lord, thank you for giving me
> some of your nature. Amen.

PERSONAL THOUGHTS

---

[43]John 3:3.
[44]2 Corinthians 5:17.

190   Supplements

> For this very reason, make every ef-
> fort to supplement your faith with good-
> ness, goodness with knowledge, knowl-
> edge with self-control, self-control with
> endurance, endurance with godliness,
> godliness with brotherly affection, and
> brotherly affection with love.
>
> 2 Peter 1:5–7 (CSB)

I take vitamin pills just in case I'm not getting
enough nutrients in my meals. My meals provide
the basics of calories, roughage, water, and fat (oils).
To stay healthy, I also need other nutrients, even if
only in small amounts. If I get a cold, some extra
vitamin C will help fight it.

Faith is all that is needed for forgiveness and
salvation, but other qualities in my life are needed
to grow into the person God wants me to be. In
these verses, the qualities form a chain of virtues,
each supplementing what came before. One dose
of a virtue is not enough. I will need daily expres-
sions of each one in bigger and bigger ways. When
a bump in life comes along, one of these virtues will
be the answer, just like that extra dose of vitamin C.

PRAYER: Lord, help me to grow in each
of these virtues. Amen.

191   Goodness

> For this very reason, make every ef-
> fort to supplement your faith with good-
> ness, goodness with knowledge, knowl-
> edge with self-control, self-control with
> endurance, endurance with godliness,
> godliness with brotherly affection, and
> brotherly affection with love.
>
> 2 Peter 1:5–7 (CSB)

In English, the word *good* is used to describe many
things. German chocolate cake is good. The book
I just read was good. My friend is a good neighbor. In this verse, the word *goodness* refers to moral
excellence.[45]

God's character is the standard for goodness.
He is the definition of *good*. Does my character
and actions reflect God's character? Are my actions
good deeds that God prepared for me to do?[46] I am
a child of God, so my character and actions should
be like my father's. We should have a family resem-
blance.

> PRAYER: Lord, teach me about your kind
> of goodness. Amen.

---

[45]The Greek word *arete* (*Strong's* No. 703).
[46]Ephesians 2:10.

192 Knowledge

> For this very reason, make every ef-
> fort to supplement your faith with good-
> ness, goodness with knowledge, knowl-
> edge with self-control, self-control with
> endurance, endurance with godliness,
> godliness with brotherly affection, and
> brotherly affection with love.
>
> 2 Peter 1:5–7 (CSB)

There is a difference between knowing someone
and knowing about someone. When I know someone, I have a relationship with him. We commu-
nicate. We observe each other's mannerisms. We
know each other's thought patterns. *Knowing about*
means I have information, but not relationship. I
know about people and celebrities whom I read
about in the newspaper or whom I see on TV, but
I know my wife and I know my friends through relationships.

Knowing about God is useful and is good to do.
I can learn about God by reading the Bible. Know-
ing Hebrew and Greek words may be helpful, but
I'm not satisfied with merely knowing about God.

A personal relationship with Jesus is what I
want. Knowing him is the way to have a joyful ful-
filling life. Prayer and obedience on my side build
our relationship. On his side, he cleanses me from
sin, he guides my life, and intervenes in my circumstances.

PRAYER: Lord, help me draw close to
you. Amen.

193   Self-control

> For this very reason, make every ef-
> fort to supplement your faith with good-
> ness, goodness with knowledge, knowl-
> edge with self-control, self-control with
> endurance, endurance with godliness,
> godliness with brotherly affection, and
> brotherly affection with love.
>
> 2 Peter 1:5–7 (CSB)

The guys at the high school Robot Club had a radio-
controlled hot rod. It zoomed across the parking
lot. It turned on a dime and would do wheelies at
the push of a button. The guy with the control box
could make it do whatever he wanted.

I have many urges in life. Hunger, hormones,
left-handedness, self-esteem, and a taste for German chocolate cake demand my attention. They
all come from myself. *Self-control* means deciding
which urges I will satisfy now, which I will satisfy
later, and which are denied. Will I exercise my "control box" over urges, or will they drive my life?

PRAYER: Lord, self-control is hard. I
need your help. Amen.

PERSONAL THOUGHTS

194   Endurance

> For this very reason, make every ef-
> fort to supplement your faith with good-
> ness, goodness with knowledge, knowl-
> edge with self-control, self-control with
> endurance, endurance with godliness,
> godliness with brotherly affection, and
> brotherly affection with love.
>
> 2 Peter 1:5–7 (CSB)

Mike decided he needed more exercise. Some of
his friends were long-distance runners, so he joined
a training program. When the program was over,
he kept running with his friends. He needed endurance to run long distances. He needed perseverance to keep training. He needed patience to
see his body develop the endurance needed for a
marathon.

Spiritual endurance[47] is sometimes necessary to
keep doing what God has directed even in the face
of sustained opposition. I can get discouraged
when results are not happening as fast as I would
like, but the reward for endurance will be obvious
at the end of the race.

> PRAYER: Lord, help me develop spiri-
> tual endurance to keep doing what you
> say. Amen.

---

[47]The word translated *endurance* by the CSB is translated *perseverance* or *patience* by other translations.

195   Godliness

> For this very reason, make every ef-
> fort to supplement your faith with good-
> ness, goodness with knowledge, knowl-
> edge with self-control, self-control with
> endurance, endurance with godliness,
> godliness with brotherly affection, and
> brotherly affection with love.
>
> 2 Peter 1:5–7 (CSB)

As I was growing up, people said I looked like my
Dad. I've noticed some subtle resemblances, too.
For example, I sunburn just as easily as he did, and
I have some of his mannerisms.

Godliness means being like God. Of course, God
is eternal, almighty, omnipresent, and omniscient. I
can never be those things, but I can imitate his character. He is loving. He is faithful. He is good. He is
just. He is merciful. He is pure. He is holy. The list
goes on and on.

Little by little, I've been learning the practical
implications of being like him. As I've grown as a
Christian, it seems I work on one thing at a time.
God knows how slow I am at learning his ways.
He knows I need to focus on just one new principle,
and later, I'll be ready for the next one.

PRAYER: Lord, what aspect of your character do I need to work on next? Amen.

196   Brotherly affection

> For this very reason, make every ef-
> fort to supplement your faith with good-
> ness, goodness with knowledge, knowl-
> edge with self-control, self-control with
> endurance, endurance with godliness,
> godliness with brotherly affection, and
> brotherly affection with love.
>
> 2 Peter 1:5–7 (CSB)

For many years, my mother's family had a re-
union every three years. By spending that time together, cousins developed bonds of brotherly love
that have lasted a lifetime, even though we may live
a thousand miles apart. Brotherly affection is based
on familial relationships. It grows naturally among
children in a family.

As a Christian, I am now a member of God's
family. So, I am developing relationships with others in God's family. As relationships grow, brotherly love grows. My circle of brotherly love now
spans the globe.

> PRAYER: Lord, thank you for connecting
> me with Christian brothers and sisters
> around the world. Amen.

PERSONAL THOUGHTS

197   Self-sacrificing love

> For this very reason, make every ef-
> fort to supplement your faith with good-
> ness, goodness with knowledge, knowl-
> edge with self-control, self-control with
> endurance, endurance with godliness,
> godliness with brotherly affection, and
> brotherly affection with love.
>
> 2 Peter 1:5–7 (CSB)

Angie and I barely knew each other at the time.
We were riding together to an event in my car
when suddenly I felt sick to my stomach. I pulled
over to the side of the road, opened my door, and
vomited—some on the ground and some in my car.
Angie demonstrated self-sacrificing love by thor-
oughly cleaning my car after getting me home.

Love is not just a warm feeling. It must be expressed in actions. The Greek word translated *love*
in this verse[48] is distinguished from romantic love
and familial love. In New Testament usage, Jesus
sacrificing himself, going to the cross, is the prime
example of love in action.

Jesus wants me to love others the way he loves
me.[49] In practice, that means sacrificing my conven-
ience for the benefit of others. It means cultivating
grace and peace that spill out to encourage others.

PRAYER: Lord, show me how to live
with more of your kind of love. Amen.

---

[48]The Greek word *agape* (*Strong's* No. 26).
[49]John 15:12.

198   Not unfruitful

> For if you possess these qualities in increasing measure, they will keep you from being useless or unfruitful in the knowledge of our Lord Jesus Christ.
>
>   2 Peter 1:8 (CSB)

I have two mango trees in my backyard. Some years they bear abundant fruit and other years none. They flower in early Spring and a couple of months later there are mangoes. They need nutrients and water, and the right weather. If it is too cold, the flowers might die. If it is too dry, the fruit won't mature. When conditions are right, there are plenty of mangoes for me, the neighbors, the raccoons, and the squirrels.

The virtues listed in the previous verses are fruits of the Holy Spirit working in my life. When I make the effort to cultivate them, the Holy Spirit will empower me to be successful. There will be abundant spiritual fruit to bless me, the neighbors, and perhaps the raccoons and squirrels.

PRAYER: Lord, work in my life to produce good fruit. Amen.

PERSONAL THOUGHTS

199   Nearsighted

> The person who lacks these things is
> blind and shortsighted and has forgot-
> ten the cleansing from his past sins.
>
> 2 Peter 1:9 (CSB)

I'm nearsighted in one eye. I can read with that eye
if the book is about a foot from my nose, but road
signs are just a blur. So, I've worn glasses since I
was about twelve years old.

If I am nearsighted when I look at my past,
I will remember recent events clearly, but memo-
ries of the distant past will be fuzzy. Lacking the
virtues listed in the previous verses leads to forget-
ting about God's mercy in the past. These virtues
are like my glasses, enabling me to remember God's
mercy when I was first saved and to see clearly
what he is doing in my life today.

PRAYER: Lord, help me clearly see your
activity in my life. Amen.

PERSONAL THOUGHTS

200   Confirm your calling

Therefore, brothers and sisters, make every effort to confirm your calling and election, because if you do these things you will never stumble.

2 Peter 1:10 (CSB)

I am an ice skater. It didn't happen accidentally or spontaneously. I had to practice sliding across the ice. Now I have sharp blades, skates that fit, strong ankles, good balance. I am confident that I am an ice skater. I am growing more secure every time I go skating. I am falling down less and less. I am a confirmed ice skater. I am also a confirmed child of God.

The virtues listed in previous verses don't happen accidentally or spontaneously. They take some determined effort. When I see them in my life, then I know my calling and election as a child of God are confirmed. They are evidence of God's Holy Spirit working in my life. I am secure in my mind. I am confident of my salvation, my heavenly destiny, and the grace of God in this life.

PRAYER: Lord, thank you for confirming my relationship with you. Amen.

PERSONAL THOUGHTS

201   Welcome

> For in this way, entry into the eternal
> kingdom of our Lord and Savior Jesus
> Christ will be richly provided for you.
>
> 2 Peter 1:11 (CSB)

A friendship is built on shared experiences, random acts of kindness, patience with faults, self-sacrificing generosity, and brotherly love. When my friend comes to visit, I welcome him with arms wide open, extending hospitality with a big hug and a big smile.

When Jesus returns, he will welcome believers into his kingdom. Dead believers will be resurrected and living believers will be changed into resurrection bodies. We will forever be with the Lord.[50] One who is rich in the virtues listed in previous verses will receive the commendation from the Lord, "Well done, faithful servant."

> PRAYER: Lord, I'm looking forward to
> spending eternity with you. Amen.

PERSONAL THOUGHTS

---

[50] 1 Thessalonians 4:13–18.

202 Don't forget

> Therefore I will always remind you about these things, even though you know them and are established in the truth you now have.
>
> 2 Peter 1:12 (CSB)

The kitchen was a busy place as a family with six school-age kids was getting ready for the day. It was about 50 degrees outside and a bit damp. As one of the younger boys dashed out the door, Mom reminded him, "Don't forget your coat." He yelled back, "It's boiling out, Mom!" After a bit of negotiation, he reluctantly went off with his coat.

I need reminders of what the Bible teaches. Even though Sunday School gave me a good foundation, I still need to refresh my memory. Sermons, books, and personal study all help. Peter's second letter to Christians is a reminder, too.

> PRAYER: Lord, thank you for all the reminders of your Word you put in my life. Amen.

PERSONAL THOUGHTS

203 Memorabilia

> I think it is right, as long as I am in this
> bodily tent, to wake you up with a re-
> minder, since I know that I will soon lay
> aside my tent, as our Lord Jesus Christ
> has indeed made clear to me. And I will
> also make every effort so that you are
> able to recall these things at any time af-
> ter my departure.
>
> 2 Peter 1:13–15 (CSB)

I have a box of items that remind me of milestones
in my life, memorabilia. There is a plate with a picture of the church I attended in college, the slide
rule I used in college, coffee cups from places I
worked, and so on.

Peter's letter is memorabilia to remind me of his
love for our savior and what I need to know to grow
to spiritual maturity. He wanted me to learn my
lessons well, so I can recall these truths. More than
1,900 years have passed since he died, and I am
reading his memorabilia letter and applying it to
my life.

> PRAYER: Lord, thank you for reminders
> to help me grow spiritually. Amen.

PERSONAL THOUGHTS

204   Myths

> For we did not follow cleverly contrived
> myths when we made known to you
> the power and coming of our Lord Jesus
> Christ; instead, we were eyewitnesses of
> his majesty.
>
> 2 Peter 1:16 (CSB)

When I was a teenager, I enjoyed reading stories about the gods of the ancient Greeks. The Bible makes it clear there is no other god besides the creator of the universe. I knew the Greek myths were not history.

Atheists today think the stories of what Jesus said and did are myths which never happened. Peter testified he saw the glorified Lord Jesus on the mount of transfiguration and also the resurrected Christ.[51] Peter was an eyewitness. The gospel stories are not myths someone made up. I am confident Jesus rose from the dead in power and majesty. I don't need to debate an atheist over whether Jesus was just a myth.

> PRAYER: Lord, thank you for reliable witnesses of your power and glory. Amen.

---

[51] Mark 9:2–3 and 1 Corinthians 15:5 where *Cephas* is another name for Peter.

205   Son of God

> For he received honor and glory from
> God the Father when the voice came
> to him from the Majestic Glory, saying
> "This is my beloved Son, with whom I
> am well-pleased!" We ourselves heard
> this voice when it came from heaven
> while we were with him on the holy
> mountain.
>
> 2 Peter 1:17–18 (CSB)

From time to time, my Dad and I would meet someone on the street or while shopping. He would in-
troduce me to his friend. "This is my son, Ed."

When Jesus was transfigured on the mountain,[52]
Peter saw it with his own eyes and heard a voice
from heaven. God the Father confirmed Jesus is his
Son. The ministry, death, and resurrection of Jesus
fulfilled God's plan. Forgiveness of sin is available
to mankind. I am forgiven. The Father is delighted
in his son.

> PRAYER: Heavenly Father, thank you for
> sending Jesus, your son. Amen.

---

[52]Matthew 17:1–8.

206   Confirmed

> We also have the prophetic word strongly confirmed, and you will do well to pay attention to it, as to a lamp shining in a dark place, until the day dawns and the morning star rises in your hearts.
>
> 2 Peter 1:19 (CSB)

I received an email from friends saying "We are coming to visit you!" My wife and I were excited, even though the visit was months away. Finally, the day arrived. The letter was confirmed when they drove into our driveway.

The authors of the Old Testament were prophets because they spoke for God. They often spoke about the coming Messiah. The transfiguration and resurrection of Jesus confirmed what the prophets had foretold. Jesus is the Messiah, the Son of God. He is alive. He has the majesty of heaven.

> PRAYER: Lord, thank you for sending the Old Testament prophets who predicted the Messiah's coming. Amen.

PERSONAL THOUGHTS

207   Dawn

> We also have the prophetic word
> strongly confirmed, and you will do
> well to pay attention to it, as to a lamp
> shining in a dark place, until the day
> dawns and the morning star rises in
> your hearts.
>
> 2 Peter 1:19 (CSB)

I have a small flashlight that helps me get around
the house at night without stumbling. Its light is
limited to a small area just in front of me. When
the dawn shines in the window, the whole room is
visible. Not only can I see for my next step, but I
can see chairs, pictures on the walls, and the whole
path to the refrigerator.

The Old Testament prophecies about the Messiah were vague and incomplete like the way a
small lamp lights a room. When Jesus walked
among the disciples, full disclosure of the Messiah
was evident by all he did and said. He was like the
sunshine at dawn, wiping away the darkness.

PRAYER: Lord, thank you for wiping
away my darkness. Amen.

PERSONAL THOUGHTS

208 Interpretation

> Above all, you know this: No prophecy
> of Scripture comes from the prophet's
> own interpretation, because no prophe-
> cy ever came by the will of man; instead,
> men spoke from God as they were car-
> ried along by the Holy Spirit.
>
> 2 Peter 1:20–21 (CSB)

I have opinions. I might tell the world on Facebook,
Twitter, or a blog. My opinions are passionate, because they are mine. Some people have passionate
opinions about religion. "I think God wants such-
and-such." They are giving their human interpretation of events.

The Bible is not just passionate opinions. The
Jewish community, and later, the Christian community, determined which writings were inspired by
God and thus, which belong in the canon of Scripture.[53] The process took several hundred years to
arrive at a consensus. Some books of the Bible were
recognized and accepted as authoritative immediately and others were accepted over time. I accept
their consensus regarding the Bible. The inspiration
of the Scriptures is also confirmed when I read the
Bible, because it gives me life.

PRAYER: Lord, thank you for the Bible.
Amen.

---

[53]F.F. Bruce, *The Canon of Scripture* (Downers Grove, Illinois:
InterVarsity Press, 1988).

209   Men spoke from God

> Above all, you know this: No prophecy
> of Scripture comes from the prophet's
> own interpretation, because no prophe-
> cy ever came by the will of man; instead,
> men spoke from God as they were car-
> ried along by the Holy Spirit.
>
> 2 Peter 1:20–21 (CSB)

When I talk with my sister on the phone, I frequently say, "Tell your kids we love them." So later
she tells them. When God talked with Moses, Isa-
iah, or Peter, he did the same thing. "Tell my people
I love them."

The authors of the Bible were inspired by the
Holy Spirit as they spoke and wrote. God wanted
us to know the things in the Bible, so he moved
men to write it. He also has worked through men to
preserve manuscripts and to translate the Bible into
many languages. Uncertainties over manuscripts
and translations are insignificant compared to the
undeniable essence of the gospel. Jesus, the Son of
God, gave his life to save mankind from sin. He
died on the cross, rose from the dead, and will return to judge the living and the dead. It is true.

> PRAYER: Lord, thank you for preserving
> the gospel message. Amen.

210   False teachers

> There were indeed false prophets among the people, just as there will be false teachers among you. They will bring in destructive heresies, even denying the Master who bought them, and will bring swift destruction on themselves.
>
> 2 Peter 2:1 (CSB)

A chicken stew is made from cut up chicken and vegetables. The broth is delicious. Sometimes when I get a piece of chicken, I bite into it and discover a bone. Instead of complaining, I just eat the meat and spit out the bone.

Peter warned his readers to beware of false teachers. Their motives were impure. Their doctrines destroyed faith and godly living. False teachers are around today, too, so I must be careful who I listen to.

Anyone can have mistaken doctrinal ideas or impure motives, even famous respected teachers. True humble followers of Jesus will always be open to correction from the Word of God. Whenever I listen to Christian teachers, I just "eat the meat and spit out the bones."

PRAYER: Lord, give me insight to recognize false teachers. Amen.

211   Destructive heresies

> There were indeed false prophets among the people, just as there will be false teachers among you. They will bring in destructive heresies, even denying the Master who bought them, and will bring swift destruction on themselves.
>
> 2 Peter 2:1 (CSB)

When I was a kid, my friend and I liked to climb the mulberry trees to get some berries. I said to myself, "That branch looks strong enough to hold me." When it started to crack, I found out that idea was a destructive heresy.

A *heresy* is a false doctrine. Destructive heresies lead people away from following Jesus. Many heresies substitute religious duties for faith and obedience to the Word of God. Some heresies substitute personal preferences for God's revelation of himself.

I am responsible for honestly evaluating my understanding of doctrine in light of the Bible. My fellow believers will help me.

> PRAYER: Lord, thank you for sending mature believers to me who correct my mistaken ideas about you. Amen.

212   Mistaken ideas

> There were indeed false prophets among the people, just as there will be false teachers among you. They will bring in destructive heresies, even denying the Master who bought them, and will bring swift destruction on themselves.
>
> 2 Peter 2:1 (CSB)

Did you know the Bible is against guitar playing? Psalm 37:1 (KJV) says, "Fret not thyself because of evil doers." Fretting on guitar must be bad...It's pretty easy to get mistaken ideas about the Bible.

A faithful disciple of Jesus may not know the Bible very well. He may be mistaken about what the Bible means. He may be deceived by a false teacher. Even if a destructive heresy floated through his brain and out of his mouth, I am still responsible to love him with self-sacrificing love. Hatred for fellow believers is never justified, even if they do have mistaken ideas.

PRAYER: Lord, give me grace for believers with mistaken ideas. Amen.

PERSONAL THOUGHTS

213   Followers of false teachers

> Many will follow [false teachers'] de-
> praved ways, and the way of truth will
> be maligned because of them.
>
> 2 Peter 2:2 (CSB)

When I was a kid, we played follow-the-leader. We would line up, and do all the silly motions that the leader at the head of the line did. If someone couldn't follow, then he was out. The one remaining when everyone else was out became the new leader.

I shouldn't be surprised that false teachers attract large crowds of devoted followers. Some false teachers become popular because celebrities are followers. Some become popular because they let followers live however they want. Some become popular because their performances are entertaining.

I don't have to follow a teacher just because he is popular, attractive, or entertaining. I must follow the Lord and the way of truth taught by the Bible.

PRAYER: Lord, help me recognize why a teacher is popular. Amen.

PERSONAL THOUGHTS

214   Truth maligned

> Many will follow [false teachers'] de-
> praved ways, and the way of truth will
> be maligned because of them.
>
> 2 Peter 2:2 (CSB)

In the 1980s, several famous televangelists were
discovered to have sexually immoral private lives
or were mismanaging their ministries for personal
gain. A few went to jail for it. These cases were
embarrassing to the Christian community, because
their lives did not reflect the gospel, even though
their preaching may have been okay.

When false teachers claim to be Christians but
live greedy immoral lives, supporting extravagant
lifestyles, secular people think that all Christians
are that way and that Jesus taught his disciples to
live that way. When unbelievers voice such opinions, the "way of truth is maligned."

PRAYER: Lord, help me live so the truth
of the gospel is not maligned. Amen.

PERSONAL THOUGHTS

215   Exploitation

> [False teachers] will exploit you in their
> greed with made-up stories. Their con-
> demnation, pronounced long ago, is
> not idle, and their destruction does not
> sleep.
>
> 2 Peter 2:3 (CSB)

I was a visitor. I noticed the pastor was not preaching from the Bible and there seemed to be an obliga-
tion to give money every service. The pastor was a
good singer and had a dynamic manner in the pul-
pit, but that did not make him a godly teacher.

False teachers are often motivated by greed.
They exploit the people of God with fund rais-
ing campaigns that are personally enriching, taking offerings at every turn, pleading in newsletters
for contributions, and manipulating listeners. Accountability for funds and their use is often lacking.

My guard is up. I will not be deceived nor ex-
ploited by false teachers.

> PRAYER: Lord, help me recognize when
> a false teacher is exploiting the flock.
> Amen.

PERSONAL THOUGHTS

216   Guaranteed punishment

> For if God didn't spare the angels who
> sinned but cast them into hell [Tartarus]
> and delivered them in chains of ut-
> ter darkness to be kept for judgment;
> ...then the Lord knows how ...to keep
> the unrighteous under punishment for
> the day of judgment, especially those
> who follow the polluting desires of the
> flesh and despise authority.
>
> 2 Peter 2:4–10 (CSB)

Every kid knows the concept of guaranteed punishment. Mom might say, "Sit in the corner now, until your father comes home." Sitting in the corner
is temporary punishment preventing further mischief, but the spanking by Dad will be the real punishment.

Peter gave three illustrations of God's power to
guarantee judgment of evil. The imprisonment of
angels who sinned is the first illustration.[54] They
are awaiting final judgment. Similarly, judgment of
false teachers is guaranteed. This is a good reason
for me to avoid associating with false teachers.

PRAYER: Lord, I know you have guaranteed punishment for evil. Amen.

---

[54]No one is sure what incident Peter is referring to. *Tartarus*
was conceived by the Greeks as a place for punishment of evil
which was lower than *Hades*, the place of the dead. The book
of Revelation calls the place where demons are confined as the
abyss and the *bottomless pit*. Blum, "2 Peter," p. 278.

217 Rescued

> And if [God] didn't spare the ancient
> world, but protected Noah, a preacher
> of righteousness, and seven others,
> when he brought the flood on the world
> of the ungodly; ... then the Lord knows
> how to rescue the godly from trials.
>
> 2 Peter 2:5–9 (CSB)

While working for a defense contractor, I realized
the contractual situation around me was becoming
more and more corrupt. I was praying for a graceful
way to let go of my responsibilities and to find a
new work environment. Then my father suddenly
died, and I had to move a thousand miles to be near
my mother. The Lord answered my prayer about
work with a much more radical change in my life
than I expected.

The second illustration of God's judgment is
Noah's flood.[55] God destroyed the corruption of the
land, but saved Noah and his family. If God judged
the corruption of that time, he is will surely judge
false teachers today, and if God rescued Noah,
he knows how to rescue me from corrupt circumstances.

PRAYER: Lord, thank you for rescuing
me from a corrupt job situation. Amen.

---

[55]Genesis 6:5–9:17.

218   No compromise

> And if [God] reduced the cities of Sod-
> om and Gomorrah to ashes and con-
> demned them to extinction, making
> them an example of what is coming to
> the ungodly; and if he rescued righte-
> ous Lot, distressed by the depraved be-
> havior of the immoral... the Lord knows
> how to rescue the godly from trials and
> to keep the unrighteous under punish-
> ment for the day of judgment, especially
> those who follow the polluting desires
> of the flesh and despise authority.
>
> 2 Peter 2:6–10 (CSB)

In college, I had many friends and neighbors who
engaged in sexual immorality, binge drinking, and
pot parties (marijuana). I knew I could not compromise my faith, yet I tried to be a friend and good
neighbor to everyone. It was difficult.

Sexual immorality was commonplace in Sodom
and Gomorrah. If the judgment of Sodom and Gomorrah was guaranteed, then false teachers who act
like them will surely face judgment, too.

Peter commended Lot, because he did not compromise. God's angels saved Lot's family from the
city's impending destruction.[56] If God did that for
Lot, he can rescue me when I do not compromise
with the immorality around me.

> PRAYER: Lord, help me resist the temp-
> tation to compromise. Amen.

---

[56]Genesis 19:1–29.

219 Fake exorcists

> Bold, arrogant people! [False teachers]
> are not afraid to slander the glorious
> ones; however, angels, who are greater
> in might and power, do not bring a slan-
> derous charge against them before the
> Lord.
>
> 2 Peter 2:10–11 (CSB)

Glorious ones in this verse may refer to fallen angels
(demons).[57]   Apparently, the false teachers were
pretending to be exorcists.

I have seen believers cast out demons result-
ing in positive changes for the victim. However, I
have also seen some who wanted to be exorcists.
They shouted and reviled demons, cursed them,
and went on and on dramatically. I'm not sure the
demons paid attention. Shouting is not what casts
a demon out. The authority of Jesus is the source of
real power over demons.

> PRAYER: Lord, give me spiritual discern-
> ment, so speaking with your authority
> will produce positive results. Amen.

---

[57]Commentators do not agree on who the *glorious ones* are.
The NIV translates the phrase as *celestial beings*. Blum, "2 Peter," p. 280.

220   Heavenly etiquette

> Bold, arrogant people! [False teachers]
> are not afraid to slander the glorious
> ones; however, angels, who are greater
> in might and power, do not bring a slan-
> derous charge against them before the
> Lord.
>
> 2 Peter 2:10–11 (CSB)

The team's mascot was dressed up as a tiger. He
boxed in the air as if he was beating up an opposing
football player. Every 300 pound lineman knows it
is not proper etiquette to fight an opposing mascot.
The mascot is not in the game.

Angels don't slander demons, but the false
teachers did. God doesn't need anyone to tell him
about the evil deeds of demons. Their judgment
is guaranteed. When compared to angels, the false
teachers were obviously arrogant, and had no idea
what is proper etiquette in heaven's court.

PRAYER: Lord, teach me proper etiquette
for your presence. Amen.

PERSONAL THOUGHTS

221   Be careful

> But these [false teachers], like irrational animals—creatures of instinct born to be caught and destroyed—slander what they do not understand, and in their destruction they too will be destroyed. They will be paid back with harm for the harm they have done.
>
> 2 Peter 2:12–13 (CSB)

Internet video production has become so economical that practically anybody can have a video program for the world to see. You too can easily learn how to be an Internet video sensation. Similarly, the cost of self-publishing books has dropped to almost nothing. Consequently, anybody can teach without accountability. It doesn't matter how weird the doctrine is.

Teachers who separate themselves from the rest of the Christian community or who criticize other ministries angrily are in danger of becoming like the false teachers Peter described. Such teachers are often preoccupied with small points of doctrine, belaboring things they don't understand themselves.

PRAYER: Lord, I will be careful whom I listen to. Amen.

222 Feasting

[False teachers] consider it a pleasure to carouse in broad daylight. They are spots and blemishes, delighting in their deceptions while they feast with you.

2 Peter 2:13 (CSB)

During the Sunday morning service, a first-time visitor asked permission to "testify." It turned out to be a mini-sermon and giving personal prophecy (exhortations) to members of the congregation. I think the church leaders were naive that day. Fortunately, in this case, no bad consequences were obvious.

Events at most churches are open to the public, so any worldly person is welcome. We hope that sinners will repent and that unaffiliated Christians will join us. However, most churches don't test the profession of visitors.

Peter noticed the false teachers were feasting with believers. Even though they had worldly parties, they pretended to be sincere Christians. Believers today must be careful. I surely don't want to embrace a false teacher.

> PRAYER: Lord, when I'm leading a meeting, I will be cautious whom I invite to speak. Amen.

223   Eyes of immorality

> [False teachers] have eyes full of adul-
> tery that never stop looking for sin. They
> seduce unstable people and have hearts
> trained in greed. Children under a curse!
> 2 Peter 2:14 (CSB)

Some guys look at every girl or woman they meet
through a sexual lens, evaluating what kind of sex
object she would be. This is a standard attitude in
the world. Some in church are like this, too. Not
everyone in church has a sanctified mind.

Jesus said if a man looks at a woman with lust,
he has already committed adultery in his heart.[58]
Peter said these false teachers did this all the time,
and would put those immoral thoughts into action
at a moment's notice. A false teacher's sermon may
not be incorrect, but his actions will corrupt believers.

> PRAYER: Lord, I will carefully evaluate
> the actions and attitudes of teachers in
> my life. Amen.

PERSONAL THOUGHTS

---

[58]Matthew 5:28.

224 Greed

> [False teachers] have eyes full of adultery that never stop looking for sin. They seduce unstable people and have hearts trained in greed. Children under a curse!
>
> 2 Peter 2:14 (CSB)

My sister and I played the board game Monopoly with our friends. The goal of the game was to become so rich I could make everyone else go bankrupt. Some people make a game of trying to make a fast dollar from any situation in life.

The word *trained* implies an athletic workout. The false teachers Peter described were so greedy that their skill was like an athlete who trains for his sport. If one practices, one becomes an expert. If one is greedy at every turn of life, then he becomes an expert in how to take advantage of every situation for financial profit. False teachers like that will corrupt the believers.

PRAYER: Lord, help me root out greedy attitudes in my life. Amen.

PERSONAL THOUGHTS

225 Wages of unrighteousness

> [False teachers] have gone astray by
> abandoning the straight path and have
> followed the path of Balaam, the son of
> Bosor, who loved the wages of wicked-
> ness.
>
> 2 Peter 2:15 (CSB)

Balaam was a non-Israelite prophet of the Lord.[59]
When Moses and the Israelites approached Moab,
Moab's king, Balak, tried to hire Balaam to curse
the Israelites. Balaam wanted the honorarium that
Balak was willing to pay, but the Lord would not
let Balaam speak a curse. The false teachers Peter
criticized were greedy. Following Balaam's example, they would gladly speak against someone if the
price was right.

Some Christian teachers today seem to specialize in stirring up controversy. They accuse a Christian in the public eye of heresy, or criticize worldly
people in popular culture or politics. For a TV
ministry, controversy attracts a big audience which
translates into more contributions, more advertis-
ing revenue, and more sales of books and videos.

Criticism without relationship doesn't result in
repentance, and majoring in minor issues without
Christian love is not the Jesus way.

> PRAYER: Lord, give me love for fellow
> believers who major in minor issues.
> Amen.

---

[59]Numbers 22:1–24:25.

226   Donkey

> But [Balaam] received a rebuke for his
> lawlessness: A speechless donkey spoke
> with a human voice and restrained the
> prophet's madness.
>
> 2 Peter 2:16 (CSB)

As Balaam traveled to his well-paying prophecy
job, his donkey saw an angel with a sword in
their path, and so the donkey refused to go further.
When Balaam beat the donkey, the donkey replied
and explained the situation.[60]

Sometimes I hear the word of the Lord from an
unexpected source. Perhaps a worldly unbeliever
makes a casual remark. Perhaps a child explains a
biblical truth. Perhaps I see a billboard on the the
roadside. Any of these might trigger a word in my
spirit. If I'm being rebellious, the Lord may need to
use a radical method to get his word of correction
into my head.

> PRAYER: Lord, I am listening for your
> word for me, even it it is from an un-
> likely source. Amen.

PERSONAL THOUGHTS

---

[60]Numbers 22:22–33.

227 Dry springs

> These [false teachers] are springs with-
> out water, mists driven by a storm. The
> gloom of darkness has been reserved for
> them.
>
> 2 Peter 2:17 (CSB)

It was a hot summer day at the park. I was thirsty.
I noticed a water fountain across the field in the
picnic area. So I marched right over there to get a
drink. When I pushed the button on the fountain,
only a dribble came out. It looked like a promise of
refreshment, but was actually a disappointment.

At first glance, a false teacher seems to be offering spiritual refreshment, but he is actually dry.
Even though a teacher is famous, his many eloquent
words may be empty.

PRAYER: Lord, help me recognize empty
teaching. Amen.

PERSONAL THOUGHTS

228   Boastful

> For by uttering boastful, empty words,
> [false teachers] seduce, with fleshly de-
> sires and debauchery, people who have
> barely escaped from those who live in
> error.
>
> 2 Peter 2:18 (CSB)

A guest speaker from across town visited a home
Bible study I attended. He boasted of miracles on
mission trips and how a famous author was a personal friend. I assume the guy was sincere, but
based on Peter's warning, I wouldn't invite him
again.

The false teachers Peter described taught that
greed and sexual immorality are okay. Their victims were new believers who recently escaped a
worldly lifestyle and the mistaken ideas that go
with it. A false teacher seems so confident. A Christian teacher who mostly talks about his accomplishments or the famous people he knows is not to be
trusted.

PRAYER: Lord, I won't trust an arrogant
teacher. Amen.

PERSONAL THOUGHTS

229   Slaves of corruption

> [False teachers] promise them freedom,
> but they themselves are slaves of corrup-
> tion, since people are enslaved to what-
> ever defeats them.
>
> 2 Peter 2:19 (CSB)

Jim and Dan hunted feral pigs out in the woods. (Wild pigs are considered a pest.) When they killed one, they would butcher it and have plenty of pork to eat at home. They built a trap to catch pigs while they couldn't be out in the woods. The trap caught several piglets. So Jim and Dan provided food and water for them. The piglets probably thought life was good. They were free to eat and drink, but in the end, they were destined for the dinner table.

When a Christian teacher falls into greed or sexual immorality, he's lost his insight about freedom. Sin enslaves. He might make excuses, claiming to have "freedom to do what I want." But true freedom is the power to live righteously without being drawn into sin.

> PRAYER: Lord, thank you for the free-
> dom you give. Amen.

PERSONAL THOUGHTS

230   Again entangled

> For if, having escaped the world's impurity through the knowledge of the Lord and Savior Jesus Christ, [false teachers] are again entangled in these things and defeated, the last state is worse for them than the first.
>
> 2 Peter 2:20 (CSB)

Rock and roll had been a big part of Angie's life in the world. So shortly after becoming a Christian, she threw away her extensive music collection. She was determined not to be entangled again.

The false teachers Peter described became entangled by the worldly lifestyle they previously had before hearing the gospel. I must guard my thoughts and actions to avoid worldly ways from which I have been delivered. I don't want to go back to old sins and patterns. I'll quickly repent if I tiptoe in that direction.

PRAYER: Lord, help me avoid my old worldly patterns. Amen.

PERSONAL THOUGHTS

231 Ignoring the gospel

> For it would have been better for [false
> teachers] not to have known the way of
> righteousness than, after knowing it, to
> turn back from the holy command deliv-
> ered to them.
>
> 2 Peter 2:21 (CSB)

Some Bible teachers emphasize a minor point of
Scripture so much that the gospel is ignored. Cat-
egories include social justice, end-times prophecy,
personal prophecy, popular culture, spiritual war-
fare, miracles, visiting heaven, and so on. These are
all legitimate topics, but they are not the core of the
gospel.

In this verse, Peter continued to condemn false
teachers. The false teachers were ignoring the core
of the gospel. Even though they understood the
gospel, they were corrupting God's people. It
would have been better if they had remained pagans, because then God's people would have ignored them.

Of course, I don't listen to leaders of recognized
cults, but I also tune out those who emphasize minor issues. I will focus on the core of the gospel and
keep other topics in proper perspective.

> PRAYER: Lord, give me your perspec-
> tive on the importance of various topics.
> Amen.

232   Wallowing in the mud

> It has happened to [false teachers] according to the true proverb: "A dog returns to its own vomit," and, "A washed sow returns to wallowing in the mud."
>
> 2 Peter 2:22 (CSB)

A couple had divorced due to the husband's drug addiction. He claimed to have become a Christian, so he and I had weekly one-on-one Bible studies. After a while, it became evident he was really just interested in having sex with his ex-wife. He also went back to doing drugs.

False teachers' true nature eventually will be revealed. Peter said they returned to the "mud" of greed and immorality that had enslaved them when they were pagans. You can wash a pig for show at the county fair, but it will jump in the mud at first opportunity.

> PRAYER: Lord, give me your insight into false teachers I encounter. Amen.

PERSONAL THOUGHTS

233 Reminders

> Dear friends, this is now the second let-
> ter I have written to you; in both let-
> ters, I want to stir up your sincere un-
> derstanding by way of reminder, so that
> you recall the words previously spoken
> by the holy prophets and the command
> of our Lord and Savior given through
> your apostles.
>
> 2 Peter 3:1–2 (CSB)

"I forgot about our appointment," is one of the most
embarrassing confessions I have had to make. I
don't have any excuses. I have a calendar. Our appointment is clearly marked. But I must look at the
calendar if I'm going to keep my appointments. The
calendar is my reminder, but I must pay attention to
it.

Peter wanted his letters to remind believers
about what the Old Testament says and what our
Lord Jesus said. They learned what Jesus said from
eyewitnesses. We have the gospel writers and the
rest of the New Testament. The whole Bible is our
reliable source of information about God's character, his plans, and his actions. My grandmother had
a daily appointment with her Bible. I will imitate
her. I must read the Bible to be reminded of God's
love for me and the instructions Jesus gave us.

> PRAYER: Lord, help me to consistently
> read your Word and to apply it to my
> life. Amen.

234   Scoffers

Above all, be aware of this: Scoffers will come in the last days scoffing and following their own evil desires.

2 Peter 3:3 (CSB)

Some make fun of the Bible and the gospel, asserting that it is just stories someone made up long ago. You can find books by skeptics in the bookstore and in the library. Some such authors are scholars from seminaries and Religion Studies departments at universities. When one observes their lives and read between the lines of their books, they just want to live selfishly. They ignore God's justice and mercy, making excuses.

The scoffer I encounter may be a relative, a friend, a teacher, or someone on TV. I am prepared because Peter warned me about such people.

PRAYER: Lord, give me insight to recognize scoffers. Amen.

PERSONAL THOUGHTS

235   All things continue

> [Scoffers say], "Where is his 'coming'
> that he promised? Ever since our an-
> cestors fell asleep, all things continue as
> they have been since the beginning of
> creation."
>
> 2 Peter 3:4 (CSB)

Carl Sagan hosted a PBS[61] television series, Cosmos. He is famous for saying, "The cosmos is all
that is or was or ever will be." God's purposeful
intervention in history was inconceivable to him.

Today, more than ever, scoffers claim Jesus is not
coming back. They assume there will be no final
accounting for what each person has done. They
close their eyes to God's merciful involvement in
the lives of people. They think nature is an auto-
mated machine, ignoring God's faithfulness in up-
holding creation. They don't recognize that the
moral decline of civilization will have eternal consequences. But I know God has intervened in my
history for my good.

> PRAYER: Lord, thank you for interven-
> ing in my life to save me from sin.
> Amen.

---

[61]Public Broadcasting Service (PBS), a television network.

236 Pretending

> [Scoffers] deliberately overlook this: By the word of God the heavens came into being long ago and the earth was brought about from water and through water. Through these the world of that time perished when it was flooded.
>
> 2 Peter 3:5–6 (CSB)

When I was little, I sometimes did something I shouldn't have. I hoped Mom and Dad wouldn't find out. So I pretended that nothing was wrong. Eventually, Mom and Dad did find out and judgment fell on me.

Scoffers ignore the wonders of God's creation and the past judgments of God, like Noah's Flood. God's word is powerful and purposeful. Scoffers claim that "all things continue" only because there hasn't been a flood recently. Past judgments should be a warning to people today.

PRAYER: Lord, I'm certainly paying attention to your past judgments. Amen.

PERSONAL THOUGHTS

237 Stored

> By the same word, the present heavens
> and earth are stored up for fire, being
> kept for the day of judgment and de-
> struction of the ungodly.
>
> 2 Peter 3:7 (CSB)

Terry heated his house with a wood-burning stove.
He needed a good supply of logs to get through
the winter. So he built a place to stack logs. The
rack was off the ground, so the wood wouldn't rot.
There was a roof to keep most of the rain off. The
logs were cut the same length so they would fit in
the stove. The logs were neatly stacked. Terry was
prepared for fire in the winter.

The Lord has a plan for the created order. One
day it will be time to finally get rid of sin. He plans
to use fire on the day of judgment. The ungodly
will be destroyed, but he's preparing a new world
for us who believe.

PRAYER: Lord, I'm looking forward to
your new heaven and new earth. Amen.

PERSONAL THOUGHTS

238 Timeless

> Dear friends, don't overlook this one
> fact: With the Lord one day is like a
> thousand years, and a thousand years
> like one day.
>
> 2 Peter 3:8 (CSB)

When I was little, I was eager for Christmas to arrive. The time from Thanksgiving in November to Christmas seemed like forever. Adults would say, "Christmas is right around the corner," but it didn't seem that way to me. Kid time and grownup time are not the same.

We talk of God as eternal. This verse tells us God's sense of time is different from ours. I think he invented time for our benefit. The rising of the sun marks the day. The phases of the moon mark the month. We are locked into today, but he is timeless.

> PRAYER: Lord, give me your perspective
> on human history and my time on earth.
> Amen.

PERSONAL THOUGHTS

239 Delay

> The Lord does not delay his promise, as some understand delay, but is patient with you, not wanting any to perish but all to come to repentance.
>
> 2 Peter 3:9 (CSB)

I was on my way to an appointment. I sure didn't want to be late. A train was at the railroad crossing. I wondered how many miles long that train was. Then each red light on my way made me more anxious. When I got there, the parking lot looked full. Eventually, I found a spot at the back of the parking lot. I hiked across the parking lot as fast as I could. When I got there, the secretary told me the person I was meeting had called. He was stuck in a traffic jam. People may be delayed, but God is never late.

Almost two thousand years ago, Jesus promised to come again in glory. People think two thousand years is a long time. Doubters say, "Is he really coming?" Jesus said the Father will decide when the time is right. To him, two thousand years are like just a couple of days. Nothing has blocked Jesus' coming. He's not too busy. His white horse isn't sick. His robe is not at the cleaner's. He isn't stuck in traffic. He didn't have a flat tire. He will return at the right time.

> PRAYER: Lord, it is hard to be patient when I'm eager for your return. Amen.

240   Waiting

> The Lord does not delay his promise,
> as some understand delay, but is patient
> with you, not wanting any to perish but
> all to come to repentance.
>
> 2 Peter 3:9 (CSB)

When a baby is learning to walk, Daddy will patiently wait for those feeble halting steps. He calls out, "Come to Daddy." First the baby concentrates on grabbing the chair to stand up. Then she has to turn around to see Daddy across the room. Then a step or two. Then she falls down. Then she gets up again. Then she turns around again. Then some more steps. All the while, Daddy is patiently waiting.

The Lord is waiting for people to repent. He is patient. He knows some of us take longer to make that choice. He loves all of creation, especially all people. He knows that repentance is the only escape from the wages of sin, which is death.[62] So he is patient.

> PRAYER: Lord, thank you for waiting for
> me to repent. Amen.

---

[62]Romans 6:23.

241   Thief

> But the day of the Lord will come like
> a thief; on that day the heavens will
> pass away with a loud noise, the ele-
> ments will burn and be dissolved, and
> the earth and the works on it will be dis-
> closed.
>
> 2 Peter 3:10 (CSB)

A thief always breaks into a house when no one is
expecting him. Otherwise, the homeowner would
defend his property.

The Day of the Lord will be a surprise. No one
will know when it is about to come. People will
be going about their business when suddenly the
time for accounting for every thought and action
will have arrived.

I want my life to always be clean and obedient
to the Lord. The surprise of the Day of the Lord
won't be intimidating to me. I don't care when the
Father schedules judgment day.

PRAYER: Lord, I am ready for the Day of
the Lord. Amen.

PERSONAL THOUGHTS

242   Burned up

> But the day of the Lord will come like
> a thief; on that day the heavens will
> pass away with a loud noise, the ele-
> ments will burn and be dissolved, and
> the earth and the works on it will be dis-
> closed.
>
> 2 Peter 3:10 (CSB)

The advent of the atomic bomb and later the hydro-
gen bomb revealed the awesome power God has
hidden in the atom. Explosions on our sun are even
more powerful. Astronomers have observed gigan-
tic explosions among the heavenly bodies which
make those on our sun seem small.

The heavens and earth, everything, will someday be burned up. All the evil works of this world
will pass away with them. The Lord has promised a
new place for us to replace this corrupted old place.

PRAYER: I'll be happy to see this old corrupt world pass away. Amen.

PERSONAL THOUGHTS

243   What sort of people

Since all these things are to be dissolved in this way, it is clear what sort of people you should be in holy conduct and godliness as you wait for the day of God and hasten its coming.

2 Peter 3:11–12 (CSB)

I enjoy watching people at the shopping mall. All kinds of people walk by, all shapes and sizes, all social strata, and all ages. There are little kids, teenagers, moms, and couples. The fashionistas wear their styles to let you know what group they're in. You see all kinds of family dynamics: arguments, public displays of affection, and ice cold stares. What kind of person do others see in me?

While I'm waiting for the coming Day of the Lord, God wants my behavior to reflect his holiness and godliness. Then there will be no doubt that I belong to him.

PRAYER: Lord, help me demonstrate that I belong to you. Amen.

PERSONAL THOUGHTS

244   Eager

> Since all these things are to be dissolved
> in this way, it is clear what sort of peo-
> ple you should be in holy conduct and
> godliness as you wait for the day of God
> and hasten its coming.
>
> 2 Peter 3:11–12 (CSB)

I was expecting my sister and her family to visit us
for the weekend. I planned to hug their necks, but
I had no idea when they would arrive. They don't
always leave their house on time and there could be
delays during the drive. I was eager to see them.

I am expecting to see the return of my Lord Jesus. I love him and he loves me. Life will be so
much better when he gets here. Creation will rejoice. Justice will prevail. Righteousness will spread
across this world. I want him to come right away,
the sooner, the better.

PRAYER: Lord, I am eager to see you.
Amen.

PERSONAL THOUGHTS

245   Waiting for the new

> Because of that day, the heavens will
> be dissolved with fire and the elements
> will melt with heat.   But based on his
> promise, we wait for new heavens and a
> new earth, where righteousness dwells.
>
> 2 Peter 3:12–13 (CSB)

I had a two-door coupe I thought was a sporty car.
It even had a retractable sunroof. However, when
it rained, the sunroof leaked, and water collected in
the ceiling. When I pulled out of a parking space after a rain shower, water poured down on my head.
The day I finally traded it in for a new car was one
of the happiest days of my life. By the way, the new
car did not have a sunroof. God will trade in this
old world for a new one.

The promised destruction of this world is not intimidating to us who believe. Nothing of value will
be lost. The new heavens and new earth will be
much better than the old which will be burned up.
Righteousness will be the identifying mark of our
new world.

PRAYER: Lord, thank you for preparing
a new place for us who believe. Amen.

PERSONAL THOUGHTS

246 Without spot

> Therefore, dear friends, while you wait for these things, make every effort to be found without spot or blemish in his sight, at peace.
>
> 2 Peter 3:14 (CSB)

During dinner, a spot of greasy gravy mysteriously appeared on my shirt. I had to get another shirt right after dinner. I had to apply some grease remover and scrub it before I was allowed to put it in the laundry basket. It took some effort, but it was worth it.

While waiting for the coming of Jesus and the end of the age, I may sin or have an unhealthy habit. Such things interfere with my fellowship with a holy God. I must promptly confess my sin, so I can be cleaned up. I must also break unhealthy habits. The Lord will help me. It takes some effort over time, but it'll be worth it.

PRAYER: Lord, help me keep clean in your sight. Amen.

PERSONAL THOUGHTS

247   Opportunity

> Also, regard the patience of our Lord as
> salvation, just as our dear brother Paul
> has written to you according to the wis-
> dom given to him.
>
> 2 Peter 3:15 (CSB)

The department store sent me a notice of their sale
this weekend. "This is your big opportunity! On
Friday, Saturday, and Sunday, prices will be slash-
ed, but it will be too late on Monday."

God is patient, hoping that people will repent.
It is a big opportunity to gain eternal life. He is not
destroying this old world yet, but someday it will
be too late. His patience gives you and me time to
lead some to Jesus and to live a life that brings God
glory.

> PRAYER: Lord, thank you for your pa-
> tience with me. Amen.

PERSONAL THOUGHTS

248   Scripture twisting

> [Paul] speaks about these things in all
> his letters. There are some matters that
> are hard to understand. The untaught
> and unstable will twist them to their
> own destruction, as they also do with
> the rest of the Scriptures.
>
> 2 Peter 3:16 (CSB)

One of my favorite books is *Scripture Twisting* by
James W. Sire.[63] He explains twenty ways that cults
misinterpret the Bible. I've noticed that Christians
sometimes twist the Scriptures the same way. For
example, taking a verse out of context often twists
the meaning of the passage. Even my pastor did
this sometimes. Maybe I've done it, too.

If Peter thought some of God's truths are hard to
understand, then I should not be discouraged when
I come across a Bible passage I don't understand.
When a passage is difficult, I must be careful not to
grasp at any weird interpretation that comes along.

PRAYER: Lord, help me understand the
Scriptures properly. Amen.

---

[63]James W. Sire, *Scripture Twisting: 20 Ways the Cults Misread
the Bible* (Downers Grove, Illinois: InterVarsity Press, 1980).

249 Stability

> Therefore, dear friends, since you know this in advance, be on your guard, so that you are not led away by the error of lawless people and fall from your own stable position.
>
> 2 Peter 3:17 (CSB)

When I encounter a difficult Bible passage, I read one interpretation after another, hoping to understand the passage. Bible scholars have many opinions and frequently disagree with each other. Some don't believe the Bible is the Word of God. Some think the Bible is not authoritative or reliable. I guess they don't want to obey the Bible's teachings.

I'm not going to let a difficult passage or some controversy lead me away from simple faith in Jesus. I'm secure and stable in what I do know and understand.

> PRAYER: Lord, thank you for your truth in the Bible, even though I don't understand everything. Amen.

PERSONAL THOUGHTS

250   Growth

> But grow in the grace and knowledge
> of our Lord and Savior Jesus Christ. To
> him be the glory both now and to the
> day of eternity.
>
> 2 Peter 3:18 (CSB)

I've been trying to grow some shrubs and ground cover in my backyard. During the summer rains, I don't need to do much except pull some weeds. During the dry season, their leaves curl up and they don't look well, so I get out the hose and give them a drink. They just grow at their own pace.

My growth as a Christian has been gradual along with my maturing as a person. There have been seasons when my faith was boosted by God's activity around me. There have been seasons when I felt dry. I had to dig in the Bible to find a spiritual drink. Like the shrubs in my backyard, I'm still growing.

> PRAYER: Lord, thank you for helping me grow spiritually. Amen.

PERSONAL THOUGHTS

Meditations on Jude

251   Called, loved, and kept

> Jude, a servant of Jesus Christ and a
> brother of James: To those who are the
> called, loved by God the Father and kept
> for Jesus Christ.
>
> Jude 1:1 (CSB)

The kids in the neighborhood played outside in my
yard or in the yard across the street. At dinnertime,
my mother called to me and my sister. We knew
something good was waiting for us, because she
loved us.

I was called to repent. I responded and my sins
were forgiven. My new purpose is to live as a follower of Jesus. I am loved by God the Father. I'm
a child of God. He is interested in all the details of
my life. I am secure in the faith. My eternal destiny
is guaranteed. When Jesus returns to earth, I will
join all the believers in worship.

PRAYER: Lord, thank you for calling me,
loving me, and keeping me. Amen.

252   Mercy, peace, and love

> May mercy, peace, and love be multi-
> plied to you.
>
> Jude 1:2 (CSB)

As I drove out of the parking lot, I could see a horde of cars were coming down the street. I thought I would have to wait forever to get into traffic. I was surprised when a car stopped and the driver waved for me to go ahead. He gave me mercy when he had the right of way.

Because Jesus died on the cross, I have received mercy from God. In all the ups and downs of life, he demonstrates his mercy over and over. The Holy Spirit in me gives me peace that the world cannot understand. My surroundings may be in turmoil, but I have God's peace. Forgiveness of my sin was just the beginning of experiencing God's love for me. He gives me overflowing love to splash on those around me.

> PRAYER: Lord, thank you for your mercy, your peace, and your love for me. Amen.

PERSONAL THOUGHTS

253   Contend

> Dear friends, although I was eager to
> write you about the salvation we share,
> I found it necessary to write, appealing
> to you to contend for the faith that was
> delivered to the saints once for all.
>
> Jude 1:3 (CSB)

I was the only college student in my adult Sunday
School class. I expected the older members to lead
the Bible lesson. As they talked, I realized they did
not believe the Bible was the Word of God. They
picked out the parts that made them feel comfort-
able or substituted their own ideas. I just had to
speak up.

In secular society, there are plenty of people who
oppose the gospel, but sometimes worldly ideas or
practices are advocated among God's people. Jude
advised me to "contend for the faith." In the following verses he describes the sins and judgment
for those who would corrupt God's flock.[64]

> PRAYER: Lord, give me the right words
> and the right attitude when I must de-
> fend the gospel. Amen.

---

[64]2 Peter 2:1–22 is similar to Jude 1:3–19. Peter warned of
false teachers. Jude warned of ungodly people.

254   Stealth

> For some people, who were designated
> for this judgment long ago, have come
> in by stealth; they are ungodly, turning
> the grace of our God into sensuality and
> denying Jesus Christ, our only Master
> and Lord.
>
> Jude 1:4 (CSB)

Everyone was shocked when the pastor announced that an associate pastor had fallen into adultery with a church secretary. The associate pastor repented, went through some months of marriage counseling, and remained part of the congregation. The secretary did not repent and left the church.

Church services are open to the public. Not everyone that attends is a believer. Some try to fake it, spouting Christian jargon and pretending to be devout. Jude warned about ungodly people who ingratiate themselves, but claim immorality is okay, denying Jesus meant what he said.

> PRAYER: Lord, help me recognize those
> who are trying to flatter me with religious jargon, but are just pretending to
> know you. Amen.

PERSONAL THOUGHTS

255   Unbelievers

> Now I want to remind you, although
> you came to know all these things once
> and for all, that [the Lord] saved a peo-
> ple out of Egypt and later destroyed
> those who did not believe.
>
> Jude 1:5 (CSB)

As I walked around Edinburgh, Scotland, I saw a
stately church building being used as a night club.
I wondered what happened to the congregation. If
people substitute religious motions for faith, a congregation will melt away. Without a congregation,
there is no local church.

Jude gave three examples of the judgment
awaiting those who would corrupt God's people.
The first example was judgment of those among
the Israelites who rebelled against Moses over and
over.   For example, a whole generation died in
the wilderness, because they did not believe God
would give them victory over the Canaanites.[65] If
God destroyed those unbelieving Israelites, then he
will surely destroy those who would corrupt God's
people today.

> PRAYER: Lord, I won't listen to those
> who would sow unbelief. Amen.

---

[65]Numbers 13:1–14:38.

256 Demons in chains

> And the angels who did not keep
> their own position but abandoned their
> proper dwelling, [the Lord] has kept in
> eternal chains in deep darkness for the
> judgment on the great day.
>
> Jude 1:6 (CSB)

When someone is convicted of murder, the death penalty is usually delayed. The criminal must wait in jail on death row until it's time to enforce the sentence. God is planning to enforce his sentence on corruption among his people, too.

The second example of judgment is the imprisonment of fallen angels (demons) who rebelled against the Lord.[66] They will be judged on the Last Day. Their eternal punishment is described as a *lake of fire*, reserved for the devil and all who are allied with him.[67] If God has guaranteed punishment for demons who rebelled, he will surely punish those who would corrupt God's people.

> PRAYER: Lord, I know that you will
> punish evil. Your justice is guaranteed.
> Amen.

---

[66]2 Peter 2:4. Chaining of fallen angels (demons) is not an incident in the Bible. Revelation calls the place where demons are imprisoned the *abyss* (CSB) and the *bottomless pit* (KJV) (Revelation 9:1–11; 20:1–3).

[67]Revelation 20:10.

257   Sodom and Gomorrah

> Likewise, Sodom and Gomorrah and the surrounding towns committed sexual immorality and perversions, and serve as an example by undergoing the punishment of eternal fire.
>
> Jude 1:7 (CSB)

A young professional man was a member of a home Bible study. He and his new girlfriend were in church together. Shortly after she moved in with him, they quit coming to church. I suppose he realized this church did not condone sexual immorality.

The third example of judgment is fire falling on Sodom and Gomorrah.[68] These towns were judged for their rampant sexual immorality. If God judged Sodom and Gomorrah, then he is sure to judge those who practice sexual immorality among God's people.

> PRAYER: Lord, help me to reject condoning sexual immorality among God's people, but to offer correction and forgiveness to those who repent. Amen.

PERSONAL THOUGHTS

---

[68]Genesis 19:1–25 and 2 Peter 2:6–10.

258 Slanderers

> In the same way these people—relying
> on their dreams—defile their flesh, reject
> authority, and slander glorious ones.
>
> Jude 1:8 (CSB)

A couple who led a home Bible study seemed to specialize in shouting at demons. I wasn't sure the demons paid attention. They weren't accountable to church leaders and before long, left the church. Slandering demons didn't produce good results.

The ungodly people Jude warned about thought their dreams were the source of truth. They practiced perverted sexual immorality. They rejected correction from those in authority over the church. To top it all off, apparently, in their ignorance, they were slandering demons,[69] as if they were exorcists. They were just like the rebellious Israelites, demons, and men of Sodom, and they deserved the same judgment.

> PRAYER: Lord, help me recognize and
> avoid those who are like the ones Jude
> warned about. Amen.

---

[69]2 Peter 2:10–11. Based on this passage in 2 Peter, I assume the "glorious ones" were fallen angels (demons). Blum, "2 Peter," p. 280.

259   Michael the archangel

> Yet when Michael the archangel was dis-
> puting with the devil in an argument
> about Moses's body, he did not dare ut-
> ter a slanderous condemnation against
> him but said, "The Lord rebuke you!"
>
> Jude 1:9 (CSB)

Spiritually arrogant people I've met seemed to assume that just because they are children of God,
they are able to fight the devil anywhere and any-
time. But it's foolish for a person to slander the
devil.

Jude illustrated how arrogant these ungodly
people were by explaining that the most powerful
angel did not slander the devil, but just deferred to
the Lord.[70] Certainly a human being is not qualified
to slander a "glorious one," yet these people did not
hesitate to act spiritually superior.

> PRAYER: Lord, help me keep a humble
> attitude when spiritual warfare becomes
> necessary. Amen.

---

[70]Early church fathers said Jude referred to the *Assumption
of Moses*, a non-biblical document of which only a few frag-
ments have survived. Blum, "Jude," p. 391.

260   No understanding

> But these people blaspheme anything
> they do not understand. And what
> they do understand by instinct—like ir-
> rational animals—by these things they
> are destroyed.
>
> Jude 1:10 (CSB)

Social media on the Internet seems to be an outlet
for over-caffeinated, over-opinionated, and hyper-
sensitive people who will lash out at anything they
find offensive. Jude warned about such people stirring up controversy in the church.

Instead of learning new things from others,
these ungodly people vehemently criticized anything they did not understand. Acting out of such
arrogant ignorance eventually leads to destruction.

PRAYER: Lord, help me to not over-react
to controversies at church. Amen.

PERSONAL THOUGHTS

261 Cain, Balaam, and Korah

> Woe to them! For [these ungodly people] have gone the way of Cain, have plunged into Balaam's error for profit, and have perished in Korah's rebellion.
>
> Jude 1:11 (CSB)

When I was little, I had a Bible story book that told about various people and their adventures. Some were good people and some were bad. Of course, I wanted to be like the good guys.

Jude pointed out these ungodly people have fallen into the same sins as Cain, Balaam, and Korah. Cain tried to worship without faith and fell into jealousy, hatred, and murder.[71] Balaam was greedy for a big honorarium.[72] Korah's ambition resulted in rebellion against Moses.[73] Those who are like them will face the same judgment. Cain was exiled. Balaam was dishonored. Korah was swallowed by the earth.

> PRAYER: Lord, teach me lessons from both good and bad characters in the Bible. Amen.

---

[71]Genesis 4:1–16.
[72]2 Peter 2:15–16, Numbers 22:1–35, and Numbers 31:16.
[73]Numbers 16:1–35.

262   Reefs, shepherds, clouds, and trees

> These people are dangerous reefs at your love feasts as they eat with you without reverence. They are shepherds who only look after themselves. They are waterless clouds carried along by winds; trees in late autumn—fruitless, twice dead and uprooted.
>
> Jude 1:12 (CSB)

Church people love to eat. The ladies will fix their special dishes. Angie often brings banana pudding. Tim and the guys man the grills. Everyone enjoys the fellowship. However, Jude warned of those whose selfishness corrupts the dinner-table conversation.

Jude described these ungodly people with four analogies. A reef is an unseen danger until a ship is wrecked on it. Selfish shepherds let the flock be ravaged. Waterless clouds look like refreshing rain, but are a disappointment. Dead uprooted trees cannot bear fruit. These ungodly people can have a destructive influence among the believers.

> PRAYER: Lord, help me deflect corrupt conversation at church dinners toward godly things.Amen.

263   Waves and stars

> [These ungodly people] are wild waves
> of the sea, foaming up their shameful
> deeds; wandering stars for whom the
> blackness of darkness is reserved for-
> ever.
>
> Jude 1:13 (CSB)

When a hurricane is coming, ocean waves become
big, angry, and dangerous. An extra high tide is
called a *storm surge*, which can bring destructive
surf into ocean-front homes. The waves of the sea
must always be viewed with caution.

In this verse, Jude provides two more analogies
for these ungodly people. The waves of the sea are
never stable and wash foam up on the shore. "Wandering stars"[74] are useless for navigation and might
as well be dark. These people are unstable and thus,
are ill-suited for leadership.

> PRAYER: Lord, give me insight into un-
> godly people I encounter. Amen.

PERSONAL THOUGHTS

---

[74]Planets in the night sky were called *wandering stars*, because they appear to wander relative to the other stars.

264 Executing judgment

> It was about these that Enoch, in the
> seventh generation from Adam, proph-
> esied: "Look! The Lord comes with tens
> of thousands of his holy ones to execute
> judgment on all and to convict all the
> ungodly concerning all the ungodly acts
> that they have done in an ungodly way,
> and concerning all the harsh things un-
> godly sinners have said against him."
>
> Jude 1:14–15 (CSB)

Bad behavior may be illegal, immoral, or unwise.
Society tolerates the immoral and unwise. The government only condemns the illegal, but God's justice condemns sin in all its forms.

One of the things Jesus will do when he returns
is judge everyone for what they have thought, said,
and done.[75] The truth will be exposed. Judgment
on the ungodliness of these people Jude warned
about is guaranteed with ten thousand enforcers.

> PRAYER: Lord, protect me from involve-
> ment in ungodly schemes. Amen.

---

[75]Jude quoted the *Book of Enoch*, a non-biblical document.
This quote summarizes teaching in the Bible about judgment
when Jesus returns. Blum, "Jude," p. 393.

265   Grumblers

> These people are discontented grum-
> blers, living according to their desires;
> their mouths utter arrogant words, flat-
> tering people for their own advantage.
>
> Jude 1:16 (CSB)

Churches are led by people and the pews are occu-
pied by people. It is easy to find mistakes, selfishness, and imperfections. There is always something
to complain about.

These ungodly people Jude warned about were
selfish, arrogant, and deceptive. They were never
satisfied, and they complained to anyone who
would listen.

> PRAYER: Lord, help me forgive my broth-
> ers and sisters for their weaknesses and
> love them with self-sacrificing love, with-
> out gossiping. Amen.

PERSONAL THOUGHTS

266 Scoffers

> But you, dear friends, remember what
> was predicted by the apostles of our
> Lord Jesus Christ. They told you, "In the
> end time there will be scoffers living ac-
> cording to their own ungodly desires."
>
> Jude 1:17–18 (CSB)

Scoffers today throw intellectual arguments
around, pretending to be smarter than God. They
may quote scientists, Biblical scholars, or TV
celebrities to convince themselves that the Bible
isn't true.

Jude warned of those who scoff at the Word of
God today.[76] They try to get others to join their selfish lifestyle, hoping morality is determined by majority vote. They don't want to admit a day of reck-
oning is coming when they will be held accountable.

> PRAYER: Lord, give me the right re-
> sponse whenever I meet a scoffer.
> Amen.

PERSONAL THOUGHTS

---

[76] 2 Peter 3:3–7.

267   Divisions

> These people create divisions and are
> worldly, not having the Spirit.
>
> Jude 1:19 (CSB)

When I move to a new place, I look for a local
church where the people love each other, the Word
of God is taught, and the people are growing spiritually. Controversies and disunity are symptoms of
deeper problems.

Even though the ungodly people Jude warned
about may be church members, they disrupt the
unity of the local congregation by advocating their
worldly values. Their religious rationalizations are
not from the Holy Spirit.

> PRAYER: Lord, help me preserve unity
> among believers, especially in my local
> church. Amen.

PERSONAL THOUGHTS

268   Building faith

> But you, dear friends, as you build your-
> selves up in your most holy faith, pray-
> ing in the Holy Spirit.
>
> Jude 1:20 (CSB)

When I walked the indoor track at the community center, a teenage athlete was training with an older mentor to become stronger, faster, and more agile. They marked the floor for quick footwork. They stretched. They sprinted. They they ran for endurance. They did pushups, situps, and squats. They were dedicated to building up their bodies for the upcoming season and beyond.

Instead of listening to ungodly people, I will follow Jude's advice: build my faith and pray. Talking to God about daily life and listening for direction from the Holy Spirit will build faith better than listening to scoffers.

PRAYER: Lord, help me build my faith. Thank you for listening to me. Amen.

PERSONAL THOUGHTS

269 Love

> Keep yourselves in the love of God,
> waiting expectantly for the mercy of our
> Lord Jesus Christ for eternal life.
>
> Jude 1:21 (CSB)

For a several years, my wife and I were members of an international home Bible study. There were five families from five countries, speaking five languages and attending four local churches. We experienced the love of God for each other across the differences in our backgrounds.

Jesus said if I keep his commands, then I will remain in his love.[77] He commanded me to love my fellow believers with the same self-sacrificing love that he loves me. There are all kinds of people in my local church. Some are new believers and some are mature. I must love them all. Beyond my local church I must love those in other Christian streams and traditions as well.

> PRAYER: Lord, thank you for your love. Help me spread your love everywhere I go. Amen.

PERSONAL THOUGHTS

---

[77]John 15:9–10,12.

270 Waiting expectantly

> Keep yourselves in the love of God, waiting expectantly for the mercy of our Lord Jesus Christ for eternal life.
>
> Jude 1:21 (CSB)

A strap on Angie's favorite sandals broke. Repair was impossible. This was a midsummer crisis. She ordered a pair on-line, because stores never have her size. She waited expectantly. In less than a week, the new ones arrived and fit her feet better than the old ones.

My sins are forgiven by God's mercy. My eternal life has begun, but my body is mortal. I am eagerly waiting for Jesus to return, so I will get a new resurrection body. It will fit me better than my old one and will never die.

> PRAYER: Lord, I am waiting expectantly for Jesus to return to Planet Earth. Amen.

PERSONAL THOUGHTS

271   Mercy

Have mercy on those who waver.

Jude 1:22 (CSB)

I played chess at least once a week with a new believer who was fighting drug addiction. We had long discussions about the Bible as we played. I was not offended by his many questions.

Some of my fellow believers may have doubts and questions about the faith. It is my job to be sympathetic, to encourage them, and to answer their questions as much as I can. My faith gets built up in the process, too.

PRAYER: Lord, teach me how I can help those who are wavering. Amen.

PERSONAL THOUGHTS

272   Snatching

> Save others by snatching them from the
> fire; have mercy on others but with fear,
> hating even the garment defiled by the
> flesh.
>
> Jude 1:23 (CSB)

Angie cooked a pot of spaghetti on the stove. When
it was ready, she used a towel to grab the handles.
The towel got too close to the heat and caught fire.
She snatched the towel and put the fire out at the
sink. Whew!

Satan's destiny is a lake of fire.[78] He deceives
people, hoping they will join him. If I can persuade
an unbeliever to follow Jesus, he won't end up in
the fire. Whew!

PRAYER: Lord, help me snatch friends
from Satan's deceptive grip. Amen.

PERSONAL THOUGHTS

---

[78]Revelation 20:10.

273 Standing

> Now to him who is able to protect you
> from stumbling and to make you stand
> in the presence of his glory, without
> blemish and with great joy.
>
> Jude 1:24 (CSB)

The sidewalk may not be smooth. It can be easy to trip. When a little one has a hold of Daddy's hand, an awkward step won't end in a fall. Daddy's hand will lift him up over the obstacle.

The ungodly people Jude warned about may deceive some, but God is on my side to keep me from stumbling into sin with them. God cleanses me from sin, let's me enter his presence, and gives me joy deep inside.

> PRAYER: Lord, thank you for protecting
> me from stumbling into sin with the un-
> godly. Amen.

PERSONAL THOUGHTS

274 Glory

> To the only God our Savior, through Jesus Christ our Lord, be glory, majesty, power, and authority before all time, now and forever. Amen.
>
> Jude 1:25 (CSB)

Celebrities vie for attention and renown at every gala event. The red carpet entrance is where those in glamorous clothes parade for the cameras. They bask in their fame. But human fame is fleeting.[79]

There is only one creator of the universe. He has saved me from sin through Jesus, my Lord. He deserves all the credit for the marvels of creation. His majesty is greater than any government official. He is powerful enough to make the universe.

> PRAYER: Lord, I will tell everyone who you are and what you have done in my life. Amen.

PERSONAL THOUGHTS

---

[79] 1 Peter 1:24.

275   Authority

To the only God our Savior, through Jesus Christ our Lord, be glory, majesty, power, and authority before all time, now and forever. Amen.

Jude 1:25 (CSB)

In a democracy, authority to govern is granted by the voters to the winners of elections. In a dictatorship, authority to govern is based on military power. A dictator threatens any challenger with death. God has supreme authority, because as creator, he is the giver of life.

The heavenly Father has delegated all authority to Jesus, over angels, demons, and people. There is no time limit on his reign, from before the universe began, during all of my lifetime, and into eternity.

PRAYER: Lord, you have all authority to govern my life. Amen.

Index

About the author

Edward B. Allen is the author of books for three styles of devotional Bible study. Verse-by-verse books draw devotional points from the Scripture passage in sequence. Historical-people books focus on incidents in the lives of historical people that illustrate biblical principles. Topical books explore relevant Scriptures throughout the Bible. His books also include many personal stories from modern life.

His books are in two series. Books in the *A Slow Walk* series have short meditations in daily-devotional format, such as *A Slow Walk through Psalm 119: 90 Devotional Meditations*. Books in the *Devotional Commentary* series are straight reads with a devotional slant, rather than academic or theological comments, such as *Practical Faith: A Devotional Commentary*.

He has led discussion Bible-study groups in evangelical churches for over 50 years He received a Ph.D. in Computer Science degree at Florida Atlantic University and had a career in software engineering. He has authored or coauthored over 80 professional papers.